BULLDUST
AND
DREAMS

BULLDUST
AND
DREAMS

TROY DANN

BANTAM BOOKS
SYDNEY·AUCKLAND·TORONTO·NEW YORK·LONDON

BULLDUST AND DREAMS
A BANTAM BOOK

First published in Australia and New Zealand in 1999
by Bantam

National Library of Australia
Cataloguing-in-Publication Entry

Dann, Troy.
  Bulldust and dreams : the Troy Dann story.

  ISBN 1 86325 181 2.

  1. Dann, Troy. 2. Adventure and adventurers – Australia –
  Biography. 3. Television personalities – Australia –
  Biography. I. Title.

791.45092

Transworld Publishers
a division of Random House Australia Pty Ltd
20 Alfred Street, Milsons Point, NSW 2061

Random House New Zealand Limited
18 Poland Road, Glenfield, Auckland

Transworld Publishers (UK) Limited
61–63 Uxbridge Road, Ealing, London W5 5SA

Random House Inc
1540 Broadway, New York, New York 10036

Edited by Jude McGee
Front cover photograph by Barry Skipsey
Back cover photograph by Steve Strike
Typeset in 12.5/17.5pt Bembo by Midland Typesetters, Maryborough, Victoria
Printed by Griffin Press, Netley, South Australia

10 9 8 7 6 5 4 3 2 1

To my forefathers and the many pioneers who opened up the frontier of Australia, giving us the heritage and the freedom we enjoy today. I take my hat off to you!

To my late nephew, Jacob Ryan Fogarty (who's picture appears below), and to the many sick children around the world who will never get to experience the adventure and fun of growing up in the Australian Outback. Through my book, *Bulldust and Dreams*, I hope, at least, to share some of that excitement with them.

CONTENTS

CONTENTS

ACKNOWLEDGMENTS

First and foremost, thank you to my mentors, Mum and Dad, for the continued support, inspiration and unconditional love you gave me throughout my childhood and continue to give me. You are two amazingly beautiful people with special qualities that I hope, some day, I can pass on to a family of my own.

To my sisters, Simone, Tanya and Heidi, thanks for being there for me. I love you very much.

To Nana, you are an incredible lady and a great football friend.

Thanks to my partners in crime, Brett and Uncle Scottie. You are two talented and loyal mates, and I thank God for having you as my two best friends.

Michael McGennan, you are a legend. Not only have you helped me pen 'Outback Adventures' and my feature film, *Outback Legend*, but you have been instrumental in co-writing this book with me. It's no secret the admiration I have for you. Thanks, mate.

Bill Leimbach. What can I say, good boy? Not only have you been one of my biggest supporters over the past few years but a real partner and a man with a vision for whom I have the utmost respect.

KC, Simon, Cameron, Steve and the rest of my film crew:

you are the unsung heroes behind the scenes. Thanks for your friendship, dedication and hard work. I hope we can have many more adventures together.

Jason Volbeda, you're a good man. Thanks for your great work.

Thanks to Mary Cunane for asking me to write this book. Your support has been paramount, and writing *Bulldust and Dreams* has proven to be one of the most rewarding and challenging projects I have ever taken on.

Heather Curdie and Jude McGee: it's such a joy to work alongside people with your skills and expertise. Thanks for cracking the whip and shaping *Bulldust and Dreams*.

To all the staff at Random House, thanks for your professionalism and guidance. I hope this is the start of a great partnership and friendship.

To my many fans and Outback Legends: without you this book may not have come to fruition. You are my inspiration, and I thank you dearly for your continued support.

PREFACE

I believe Australia is becoming a more and more urbanised country every day.

It seems to me we learn more about our overseas neighbours through the media and our education systems than we learn about our own back yard. We may be a young country but we have a very strong culture, and I believe we can keep it strong as long as future generations know their roots.

The famous Australian poet A.B. Paterson, Australia's Cattle King, Sidney Kidman, and the legendary Australian artist Albert Namatjira were my heroes when I was growing up. But today, kids are more likely to look up to Michael Jordan. While Michael Jordan is sending a positive message to children, let us not forget we are *Australian*, and we are *proud*. My latest hero is Steve Waugh, a true Aussie Legend!

Amburla
September 1999

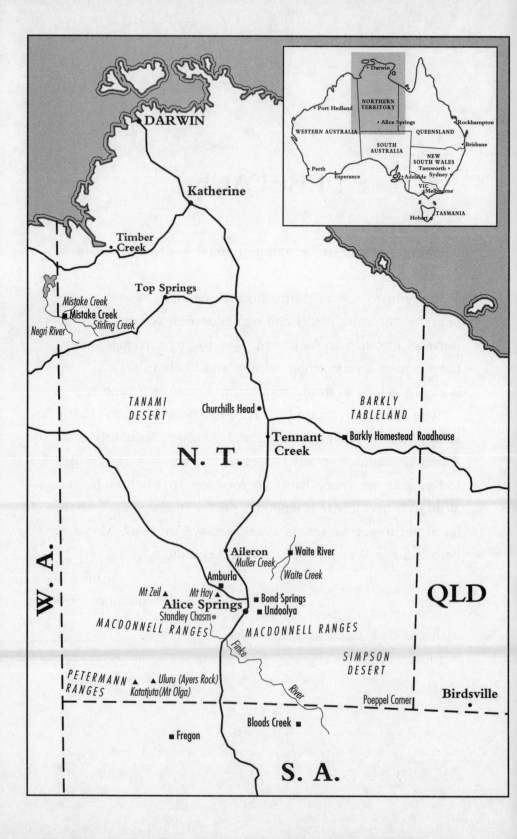

PROLOGUE

It didn't seem fair!

My life and career had taken off, with success and the promise of more to come. And always behind me was my supportive family. We'd seen each other through hard times and we'd shared the best of times.

But nothing could have prepared any of us, certainly not me, for this.

I was sitting alongside the hospital bed of my eleven-month-old nephew, Jacob. The son of my younger sister, Tanya, whom I love dearly, Jacob had been diagnosed with leukemia.

My sister and her husband, Steven, were suffering enormous pain, and my whole family was there, taking turns donating blood, saying prayers, and trying to be of as much support as we could to Tanya and her husband, Steve.

I embraced Tanya in a hug that seemed to go on forever. Over and over again she said, 'Why him? Why me?'

I had no answers except to say she was an amazing lady and that, just maybe, she'd been chosen because she had the special qualities to get through this.

I knew it didn't make sense, and I asked myself whether there really was a God. Here you have a perfect mother any kid would love to have, with a beautiful baby boy, and he's about to die. While out there how many people abuse the privilege of having a perfectly health baby?

I had prayed to God that he take my success away from me in return for Jacob's life. I offered my own life in exchange for his, so he could experience what I had experienced as a young boy. Give Jacob the years that might still lie before me.

I remember Tanya stroking her sleeping son's forehead, telling him how much she loved him. Right then Jacob opened his eyes and smiled in a way that could have lit up the whole of Sydney in a power failure or the darkest of Outback skies! He squeezed Tanya's hand in a way she had never felt before. Then, closing his eyes, he passed away.

❖   ❖   ❖

Ever since we were kids, all Tanya wanted was to have a family of her own. To bring them up on the land the way we were lucky enough to have been brought up.

You see, I don't think there is a better start for a young person than on the land, away from the problems that kids are faced with in cities.

While Jacob was in our lives, he made them richer. With his final gift of love in that tiny squeezing hand, he also gave Tanya the strength to go on.

Although Jacob will never get to experience this, I know he's with me having the adventure!

CHAPTER 1

WELCOME TO WAITE RIVER

The shadow moved.

Riding the swinging gate across the red-dust road, I could see the shape of my body, the frame and bars of the pipe-metal gate, all hard-edged black lines in the dust. But the shadow of the gate's bottom frame was shifting under my feet in a way that was all wrong.

The gate opened into our new home on a property called Waite River, 240 kilometres north-east of Alice Springs. The house and its 300,000 hectares was the hard-won prize of many years of back-breaking labour my Dad had put in working all over the Northern Territory. Now, at last, he was here, with his three kids – me, my older sister, Simone, who was seven years old, and baby Tanya – and his wife, Barbara, beside him. When Dad drove his young family up to that gate he was probably the proudest man for a thousand miles. Five thousand.

Except, by the look on his face, something right now was bothering him. I had a horrible feeling it was me.

You get to open a lot of gates on bush properties, but it's even more important to close them behind you. A small paddock in Outback Australia might be 5000 hectares with only one way in and out and no stock in sight as you walk away from a wide-open gate, but cattle have a remarkable ability to find that opening. A week's work rounding up lost stock is a big price to pay for a moment's carelessness.

But right then, at five years old, important as I knew all that was, what was more important to me as I stood standing high on the metal gate was Dad's finger pointing at me as he drove past.

You see, after I'd run up to it and unhooked it, I pushed off with one foot and rode the gate as if it were a large swing. It was at that moment, looking down, watching my own shadow sweeping across the road, that I saw the gate's shadow move in a way it shouldn't have. For a second, my eyes were fooled. But then I realised that it wasn't a shadow at all. It was a snake. One and a half metres long, at least 5 centimetres thick, and brown. Suddenly I had a better reason than sheer fun for keeping my footing on the gate.

The snake slithered over the windrow and out of sight into the short native grasses.

If Dad hadn't been saving that dark look for me he probably would have seen it, which might have been curtains for the snake. But the car slipped by, while I looked pale at having almost stepped on the biggest snake in my short life, and he looked dark-faced, as if he'd seen just about the worst example of careless behaviour ever. It was one of those moments that stay impressed upon your memory for the rest of your life.

After a quick check to make sure the snake wasn't coming back, I pushed the gate closed, placed its chain over the bolt and scurried back to the car. I opened the door and jumped in as fast as I could.

But before I had a word out, Dad had turned around and said to me, 'Son, you mustn't swing off a gate like that, ever. You'll bend its hinges and break it.'

I could see straight away he was right, and apologised. Mum smiled at me supportively. She had a way — still does — of always backing Dad up while making sure we kids know we aren't completely disgraced. Still, I couldn't contain my excitement, and words tumbled out of me about the snake I'd just seen.

Dad asked what colour it was.

'Brown,' I replied.

'That'd be right. A king brown,' he said. 'Plenty of them out here in this limestone country. Reckon I might have stayed up on the gate myself. A hinge you can fix, but a brown's venom can kill a grown man in ten minutes.'

This experience taught me something that working along-side Dad would confirm every day of my life. Dad doesn't suffer fools gladly or waste his breath where it's better spent getting something done. But you won't find a fairer man in the Territory or anywhere else I've ever been.

My father, Garry, at twenty-nine and my mother, Barbara, at twenty-six had taken on the challenges and responsibilities at Waite River Station to follow their dreams.

Right then I was as proud as a five year old can be. I'd just had an adventure that was as full of danger as daily life can be living in Outback Australia, but I'd also learnt a lesson in responsibility.

When I look back over my life, I realise that those two things have gone hand in hand right through it. Responsibility and danger. Two sides of the same coin, some people might say, but I reckon they're actually mixed in together. And not just fifty–fifty either. Sometimes you put yourself and even others in danger by not being responsible enough. Other times, by being responsible ahead of time you avoid danger altogether. The recipe changes every minute of the day, but those two ingredients are always there.

I suspect both responsibility and danger must have been on Mum's mind, too. Because, with a two year old in her lap, and a pair of roustabout kids in the back seat desperate to jump out and explore their new home, at Dad's mention of king brown snakes and their dangerous venom she let out a deep sigh. Having lived all her adult life in the bush, like every mother in Outback Australia she knew just how fragile the hold on life can be out here.

Mum was a third-generation Territorian. Her grandparents had been pioneers working on the railway line that linked up Alice Springs to the southern states. Mum had spent most holidays on her grandparents' property 200 kilometres north of the Alice called Aileron.

People think of central Australia as a hot, barren wasteland, just waiting to swallow up any living thing that puts a foot on it. Explorers have plain disappeared out here. Modern-day tourists have died of thirst and exhaustion. Whole mobs of cattle have dropped where they were standing. Families have walked off their properties with nothing but what they were carrying.

It's a tough place, no doubt about it. But Nature always has a bigger picture in mind than most of us can see. And at the centre of that picture is survival.

The most arid portion of this great continent is actually home to many species of animals and plants found nowhere else on earth. Most of them have survived here for longer than just about anything else on the planet.

I'm proud of where I live. I was born a Territorian. I expect I'll die with my boots on or I'll want to know why. But as long as I live out here I know I'll never know everything there is to know about this place. Because as surprising as Nature can be all on her own, there's nothing quite so surprising as what people get up to out here.

Waite River was a perfect case in point. Dad and a friend had bought the property off a great old Territorian Mr George Isaacson and his son. Old George was in his early eighties and was losing his sight to cataracts so it was time to sell up and move on.

Waite River had been divided into two leases and was rather small by Territory standards, but it covered roughly 780 square kilometres of some of the sweetest country around.

George had a fear of snakes, so he'd brought in some cats to keep the snakes away from the house at the very least.

Well, there can't have been that many snakes near the house, because when we pulled up outside Waite River homestead, the cats had obviously had enough time on their paws to think of things other than killing reptiles. Making more cats, to be specific. They were all over the place – all different breeds – and the smell of cat pee seemed to fill the air and waft up your nose with the slightest whisper of the south-easterly desert breeze, especially after a light shower of rain.

As Mum and Dad talked to George, Mum concentrated fiercely on the social niceties, as if that was a way to deny the smell. Simone has never been one to keep her opinion to herself, and she let Mum know straight off that the place was on the nose. Mum waved Simone and me away, and we both scooted around towards the back of the house, where I could just see the branches of a big athel tree that looked like it might need some climbing.

With one good look at it we skidded to a halt in jaw-dropping silence. There wasn't a branch on the thing, or a crook against the trunk, without its own cat. If we'd been living in a fairy tale you'd have had to call it a Cat Tree, there were so many mangy looking creatures all over it, like pears on a heavily laden fruit tree.

And weren't they sure of themselves, too? They barely bothered to look at us, most of them getting on with licking themselves in places nothing that walks on two legs can quite reach. Kings and queens of this block they were, and the rest of us could just tiptoe around as if it were some special privilege to live alongside them. There's nothing more supercilious-looking than a cat that rules the roost, and there wasn't a cat up that tree that didn't seem to think it was the only cat for a thousand miles, and the best on show to go with it.

All of a sudden, both of us heard a scream from around the house. It was Tanya. She'd been bailed up by an old one-eyed rooster. It was a mean bird, and he didn't like kids – he had probably never seen one, through one-eye or not, with George, his son and some Aborigines the only human beings out here.

Tanya was yelling away as only two year olds can. Mum came racing out of the house to see the rooster doing a side-stepping stalking dance at my sister. Mum just swept her little girl up and shooshed the rooster away.

He was obviously a character, because somehow or other he had kept his little brood of hens alive with all those cats around. That missing eye was probably due to a run-in with a cat, but even without it he was a tough old bird.

The image of that rooster must have stuck in Dad's mind. We inherited him, even after Mum's new chickens came in, and Dad would give him some of his own back, closing one eye and doing that stalk-dance straight back at him when he tried to bail one or the other of us up. We'd all be laughing watching these two stick figures circling and dashing at each other, the joker side of my dad having full reign, until the rooster decided this other bloke was maybe too big to take on, and he'd retreat.

But it was still only our first day at Waite River, and the Isaacsons had been waiting on our arrival to hand over the keys, in a manner of speaking, and go. So there wasn't much daylight between meeting them and waving them farewell. Sentiment is all right in its place, but these blokes knew where their future lay. And us? We were standing in it.

❖ ❖ ❖

Life's the best teacher, they always say. In that case my Dad's middle name must be 'Life', because just about everything I've ever learnt that hasn't got me into trouble came from him. The other times I've had to learn from my own mistakes, but even then it was mostly something Dad said or showed me that got me through.

One thing Dad never does is let grass grow under his feet. He would have loved the chance to, what with some of the dry times we've been through over the last thirty years, but if grass is scarce then there's always something else that needs seeing to. And out here there's nothing that needs seeing to more than your water supply.

So at first light next morning Dad and I were at the breakfast table and itching to get out and check the watering holes. We call it going on a bore run. The problem with sitting at any table with food on it Mum's made is you keep finding reasons to stay there. She'd have to be the best cook I know of, and when you marry that to one of Dad's sayings – 'The more you eat, son, the better you're paid' – the harder it is to stand up and push away that extra mouthful.

But it wasn't too soon after the sun had first licked the wall of our new home and Mum had given me permission to leave the kitchen table that Dad and I were walking towards the workshop, me taking nearly two steps to his one.

He was treating me as he always has: a work mate with my own responsibilities for getting a shared job done.

'Well, Troy, check the oil and water in the old four-wheel-drive, and I'll get a spare tyre,' Dad said, nodding towards the work-horse vehicle that had served him well so far. 'We'll work out where we're going to put those bought steers coming from up north.'

My job done, Dad had already tossed the spare and some fencing gear in the back, and we were driving away to visit the six main water sources that were the lifeblood of Waite River Station.

Not too far out we started to see rabbits in plague numbers, something that characterised the eastern side of the Mac-Donnell Ranges. Dad grimaced and asked me why my 'new mate' – the king brown snake – was so obviously falling down on the job.

I started in on some theory about snakes having to drag

their bellies while rabbits could run, but Dad joked that it was the speed rabbits went about making more rabbits that was the issue. There weren't enough king browns for a hundred miles to wipe them out.

The main bores on the property were Jasper, North Bore, Sheep Camp, Mulga, Muller and Homestead. Every single one of them had a gate that needed opening and shutting, and if you think I got up to ride any one of them you must reckon I'm a slow learner. I never had to meet Dad's eye once coming back to the four-wheel-drive, because he's not the sort to rub anything in, but I knew he was glad I'd learnt one lesson for good.

People often wonder why Outback people give everything a name, as each of those bores had been given. I mean, they're just glorified water taps, a city bloke might say. Well, the truth of it is, you don't just live on the land out here, you become part of it. Every hill, every outcrop of rock, every peculiarity of geography or geology gets its name like an old friend. Everyone in the family, the great extended family of Outback people, so isolated and yet so bound together by the same challenges, sharing the same hardships and joys, knows what you're talking about when you name things.

It's a language of struggle, but it's also the language of survival and achievement. When you get something done out here, and it's done well, for everyone to see, then you've just cleared your way to do the next thing that needs doing. Nobody spends too much time slapping each other on the backs or resting on their laurels, as you might if you just made a killing on the stock market or bought yourself the biggest house on the street, because time's always running against you. There's always another bore to check, the fence over the next ridge to re-strain, the mob of cattle way out in the top paddock that has to be mustered, or the grading work to push out fire-breaks, clear roads or fencelines.

Even at five years old, hardly able to see over the dashboard of Dad's vehicle, that rhythm of existence, the next job waiting even before the current one is done, was a part of me.

So, as we went from bore to bore, checking the sweet water that Waite River had trapped just 25 metres under it's dusty skin, I was actually being shown something about life. That there's always something ahead that needs doing, that nothing is too tough it should be put off till tomorrow in the hope someone else will do it for you, that if the job is yours, you do it.

I watched Dad fill his hat with water from the tank at the first bore we went to, drink out of it, and then smile as broad as I'd seen him do for some time. Right there I was learning that the work has its own rewards, rewards as real as any, more in fact, than the ones that come to you unearned. I took a draught from his hat, too, and the water was beautiful, clean and sweet. When I looked up at Dad staring out over the land that was now his, to nurture, to make productive, to hand on, one day, improved from how he found it, I could see what it was that brought people like him out here, and kept them here. His expression was a mixture of pride and measurement. I'd see it again many times over the years, and it always told me the same thing: 'What's been done is good; what's still needed doing will make it better.'

'We've got a thousand head of cattle, Troy,' Dad said. 'It's a start, a good start. And if this isn't one of the best places to do it this side of Alice Springs, I haven't met the man who could show me where is.'

I handed him back his hat. He'd explained to me on the way out that half the herd we had coming out here, 500 cattle, could run in this big paddock, all 50,000 hectares of it. The other half would be split up over another couple of paddocks. But judging from this bore, and as the day turned out, the five others, none of them would be going short of a drink if we had anything to do with it.

Dad had spent a fair whack of time making his mind up where to buy. It had been no spur of the moment decision to put down stakes here. With every mile we drove, every gate we opened (and shut), every bore we made sure was working as it should, I saw his certainty grow in him. It was at least the place he thought it was, and some more besides.

It was just after midday by the time we'd checked over the last bore, all the way seeing some of the wildlife that adds so much beauty and fascination to this part of the world. The sky filled with black cockatoos at one stage, like a ragged corner of night dragged across the brilliant blue of day. They wheeled and turned, the air sharp with their wood-sawing cries, and I was still turned around in my seat watching them through the back window when Dad tapped my shoulder.

A mob of kangaroos bounded across the track ahead of us. A healthy looking mob they were, too, with a huge red male leading the way. He still had the gloss on his hide – none of the rough patches or old scars that show a leader has been challenged by younger males for leadership of the mob and mating rights with the does. That'd come, of course: the young and strong eventually shouldering aside the old and beaten down, but right now this bloke was king of the Outback, and the look he gave us as we drove by was as if he were demanding we show him our passports for intruding on his realm.

'Thinks a fair bit of himself, that fella,' laughed Dad. 'Why shouldn't he, with a back yard of plenty like this to play around in?'

'It's our place, not his,' I remember saying, with all the certainty of a boy trying to be as tough as his old man but not yet understanding where that resilience came from.

'We all move on, Troy. Where you are right now might have your name on the title deed – that keeps the lawyers happy – but we're only looking after the place, like people have before us and others will when we're gone.'

I just glared back at the roo, and it must have worked because he bounded away pretty quick, so I only half heard Dad. But his words have come back to me, and though I've seen my own name on a title deed since, and a couple of smiling lawyers too, I'm all too aware we're only here for a short time. The land goes on forever, so respect and look after it is the rule of every day.

Another thing that seemed to go on forever was the road home. I'd been so excited about going out to see the bores it had almost slipped my mind that it was as long a trip back in as out. There was a lesson in it for me while he was at it, because even through sleepy eyelids I realised we were taking a different route home.

Dad never backtracked. Ground you've just covered shouldn't need looking at from the other side unless you haven't looked properly the first time. So Dad took us home by the fence line. He had wire and tools in the back if we came across any sections that needed fixing. The fact is, any minute of the day, there's no fence in central Australia that doesn't need fixing somewhere along it. After all, there'd be way over a million kilometres of fence out here, fencing that takes blows from cattle, roos, brumbies, the weather, you name it!

So it was home on the horizon after a couple of stops to re-strain some wire, a job out here you almost learn in the cradle, the number of times you have to do it. A fence post or two needed resetting, too.

I was glad to see the gateposts most of all, with the house just 500 metres away. We drove in past the work shed and machinery sheds, and curved around a big rainwater tank. Off to the left of it were some fruit trees at one end of a bare patch destined to be Mum's vegie garden. On the other side of the tank was the staff quarters building and some more fruit trees beyond it to give a little shade later in the day as well as grow figs and oranges.

The house was between the garden and the staff quarters, with a square of lawn along one side. Beyond the house there was the saddle shed that Mum later converted into a store. Near it were the meat shed for hanging freshly slaughtered killers, the generator shed and the chook house 50 metres away. Another 150 metres or so further out were the horse stables and a small paddock. On that side of the house there were also stock yards and a goat yard that had been turned into a milking cow pen. In the other direction, down past the second bore, was the Aboriginal camp, where our new friends and helpers set up home.

There's a sort of joke out here that before you buy a property you always look at one particular corner of it – the rubbish dump. You may be about to spend a couple of million dollars, but before you do, check out if the scrap metal dump's good (usually only worth a few thousand dollars in spare parts). If it is, well she's a winner! I probably spent a lot more time in that rubbish and metal dump than Dad did before he put down his and Mum's borrowed money, but I certainly got full value out of it.

❖   ❖   ❖

At the end of my first day at Waite River dinner was on the table in quick order, and my head on the pillow not too much later. Mum looked in just before Simone and I dropped off, and told us that she loved us and to sleep well. We slept in two single beds in the one room, with Tanya in a cot across the hall.

Simone and I talked about all we'd got done that day, me with Dad, and her helping Mum clean the place up, especially where the cats had run riot. After a few laughs we fell asleep under the new family roof. I remember, tired as we were, we wanted tomorrow to come straight away.

Meanwhile, the model for how to really get things done was having a cup of tea down the hall in the kitchen with Mum. Dad would have been talking about tomorrow, too, the both of them working out, now they had a toehold on a property of their own, what they were going to do. One thing Mum would have known: she'd be seeing a lot less of Dad than she might want to for a while yet, because ends would only be met by him working away from the block for the time being.

For the next week or so, though, there was still a pile of cleaning up to do around the house and yards. The first problem was to get rid of the cats. And they weren't about to just pack up and go if we asked them nicely.

The problem with cats is they're natural born killers. Maybe, just maybe, if you keep a cat in the house you won't see too much more than the occasional dead fly, gecko or moth it has got hold of. But out in the open, the first thing a cat does is revert to type. And type is feral because, to cats, feral is natural.

That would have been fine on Waite River if the only other living things for miles had been king brown snakes. But they weren't. As I said, there's more life in the Outback than you might think. The pity of it is that a lot of it's smaller than a cat, with no real defences against a feline's speed, claws or bloody-minded patience. So, not only on our property, but right around Australia, feral cats have killed more native creatures than anything else. In the Outback, which is a particularly fragile environment, feral cats have killed so many marsupials and native birds that are unique and special to our home that I've grown to hate them.

So while Mum cleaned and scrubbed the house, disinfecting and bleaching every inch of it to banish the smell of years of cat, Dad and the stockmen dealt with the problem outside.

After a month or two we were rid of them, except for three young ones – one grey, one ginger, and a jet black puss we called 'Midnight'. It was the only way to give the native animals a fair chance of survival in their own environment.

So, here we were, a young family on an old property, with our future before us and the most ancient landscape on the planet all around us. Would we have had it any other way? Not since the last cow jumped over the moon, anyway.

CHAPTER 2

WHAT WE'RE MADE OF

It wasn't long before I knew my way around Waite River Station. I spent a lot of time out of the house, getting to know my world as it came to me, but always sensing there was more to know and other places to see just over that flat, heat-shimmered horizon. I knew there had to be a lot out there, because Dad was always having to head out into it to make a living and keep Waite River in the family name.

Dad was a contract musterer. His job was to clean up all the wild cattle on different properties right around central Australia. A pastoralist might let a herd out in a huge paddock and not see them for months or even years, often because there was never a paddock to keep them together in the first place. Over that time, they'd range far and wide and many new calves would be born. The end result is a lot of unbranded cattle and, more importantly, as far as the cattle owners are concerned, a loss of control over the breeding program. Wild bulls are like any sort of bull: they've got cows on their minds. When you've gone to trouble and expense to breed up or buy in the best bulls to improve your herd, a few Johnny-come-latelys playing Romeo out there can wreck years of good work.

Contractors separate out these wild bulls long enough to hog-tie them, put them on a truck and send them off to market. If they're young bulls that run away, they castrate them and turn them into steers to make for good tender eating. If it wasn't for blokes like my Dad, the bloodlines of Australia's Territory-bred beef would never have reached the stage they have now, valued for their meat in some of the world's pickiest markets to our immediate north in South-East Asia and Japan.

Dad and the men would go away from Waite River up to six weeks at a time. They'd come back in, scrape the dust out of the grooves in their skin and hit town and the pub (apart from Dad – he'd be back with us), then swear never to do it again. But after another month or two in the stock camp they'd go back to town and do it all over again. The Northern Territory hasn't got the title 'Drinking Capital of the World' for nothing – its hot, you work hard and you play hard!

We valued the time we had with Dad because that's the sort of bloke he is. He changes a place by being in it, and from the way Mum hung on supporting him when he returned home from a long stint away, I reckon she figured those changes were for the better in the long run.

A man lives by his reputation anywhere the work is hard and skilled. From a very young age it was obvious to me Dad was good at his job, because he was sought after by so many pastoralists. His family had lived at Wyong near the Entrance in New South Wales before his father moved up here and started working in Outback Australia. My grandfather worked for Vesteys, a big English company that ran pastoral properties right across the Top End of Australia. In fact, they owned so much of the place you could almost walk from the west coast to the Queensland border and never leave Vestey land.

Grandad managed a few properties, ran cattle camps as a head stockman and proved to be a good bushman. In central Australia he built a lot of improvements, such as stock yards, and he opened up and developed new country.

One of those properties he managed was a place called Haasts Bluff, where my father and Uncle Scottie spent quite a bit of time growing up. He'd often drive his family to town from Haasts Bluff via the Tanami Highway north of the western MacDonnell Ranges.

It was a family ritual to stop for a cup of tea by the road on the wide open plains passing Mount Hay, on Amburla Station. Grandad set his heart on buying Amburla Station one day. Dad told me how Grandad would sip that scalding cup of tea, the steam in his eyes, but a dream glinting in them too, as he thought of how, one day he would call Amburla home.

It was never to be, because he died before he could realise his dream. Dashed dreams are something many a Territorian is familiar with. The country and the life out here can be unforgiving. You never get an inch you haven't sweated for.

It might have seemed an impossible dream to the young fella training to be a butcher, but my father is a determined bloke. I reckon every day he worked he could still see Amburla Station through a steamy haze of hot tea in his mind's eye.

Of course, he had other things on his mind, too. He was still going to school with my Mum who was one of his school friends. His apprenticeship over, he entered his trade as a butcher.

These days people call blokes who have the sort of deter-
mination my Dad has 'workaholics'. I reckon you can find
people like him all over the country, working their backsides
off to fulfil a dream that's grown too big to deny. For sure,
he'd inherited the vision from the father he'd lost, but he was
always thinking beyond that. He was set to make something
for himself by never doing less than the best the job at hand
demanded.

As one of the best butchers going he'd slaughter cattle he
had picked out himself, half a dozen beasts at a time, then bone
them up and deliver them to his customers. He even took on
digging sewage drains for people's houses 500 kilometres away
in Tennant Creek, hard-slogging work to put together the
capital for the future.

Dad would go out to contract muster other people's cattle,
heading right out to the farthest borders of their properties to
bring in the far-stragglers. Usually cash didn't change hands.
Instead, on a hand shake, Dad would barter for a portion of
the thousands of cattle he'd mustered in, building up his own
assets on the hoof and putting them on agistment. That was
until he was offered half shares in Waite River by a friend of
his, as a place to stock his cattle.

The fact is, proud as he was then – all of us were – to keep
your head above water (which is precious rare enough out
here), a land owner has to think big. It's a costly business
running stock in Outback Australia, but you quickly find the
only way to meet that cost is to get bigger. Economies of scale,
the city-taught experts call it.

But as anyone out here can tell you, the harder you work,
the harder you have to work, and Dad has always thrived on
the challenge of it.

Assets don't turn themselves into cash on a whistle either. The weather, the market shifts and changes all drastically affect cash flow. You're always planning a year ahead minimum, like business people anywhere, and paying extremely high interest, but the special conditions of working the land out here can throw the best-laid plans deep into the bottom desk drawer to gather dust.

Dad really put in the hard years when I was a kid. All that working away from home – I reckon most of that was to do with the moving around he had to do as a kid with his father. Dad's way of thinking was to put his family on a piece of land he owned and go off working for other blokes for however long it took – but all the time looking out for the next patch of land he could put his own name on.

Of course, contract mustering means being out in the swag more often than under the homestead roof. The net result in human terms is that someone has to hold the fort at home. Dad couldn't have chosen a better partner than Mum for that, and a whole lot more besides.

Mum and Dad were childhood sweethearts and I believe will remain that way till they take their last breaths. I've always seen my parents as great partners through their lives together, whether it was during the times apart or the great times when all of us were under the same roof and gathered at the same table.

Mum has a special way of filling up a house with her per-sonality. And, as they say, behind every successful man is a great woman. So the job of managing the home property and the others that started to come along fell on Mum's shoulders as much as Dad's.

If anyone knew how to get on with it in this corner of the

world it was Mum. Everything from running the house and the home block, chasing down spare parts for broken equipment, supervising the governess to make sure we kids were all right, looking after the store – the lot. She'd speak to Dad every couple of days on the Codan radio when he was away, but sometimes it could break down. The radio was the only communication we had back then: no telephones, and forget mobiles and satellite links!

If I had to give you a one-line description of my Mum I'd be pushing it to get everything I feel about her in a line from here to the boundary fence. Let's just say if there's a harder working, more determined, better house-making family-shaping all-round loving and protecting woman anywhere she's some other kid's mother, maybe yours. But as far as I'm concerned, she's definitely mine. Mum of the Year, any year, every year.

Mum was young, very attractive, full of energy, and had a love of horses. A country woman herself, her family three generations local to Outback Australia, Mum had a fair idea of what had to be done, and she made more than a fair fist of it. She was the youngest of four children to another amazing woman, my grandma Nellie Lines. Write the family history of her mum's mob and it could virtually stand in for a lot of the history of settlers in central Australia.

Of course, family history gets passed on from generation to generation as stories, which tend to grow into something bigger than they started. There are so many legends and stories floating around out here they're like good friends that keep you company, wherever you go.

The oldest legends and stories belong to the Aborigines. Central Australia is the site of so much Aboriginal myth, legend

and lore that people have to be like walking antennae sometimes. You have to pick up every signal from a place, recognise
it and respond to it.

Aborigines need travel not much more than 200 kilometres
to be out of home territory, and they'll become terribly uneasy
because, if they're not exactly trespassing, they're in another
group's special place with its own legends and myths. Before
European settlers arrived, the whole country's interwoven
myths and stories created a land so full of stories you could say
the entire place was one great story. Most people have heard
of the Dreamtime, an idyllic timeless time Aborigines look
back to as the start of all things. But, in many ways, we are
still living in a Dreamtime, where the world is held together,
as it has always been, by the stories that make sense of it, add
mystery to it and give us sign posts so we can pass through it.

Every culture has myths, legends and guiding stories, most
of them set way back in time and glossed over with distance
and so much telling and retelling they are etched deep in our
minds. Often, when we hear such a story for the first time, it
already seems somehow familiar.

In Outback Australia, as well as the myths from the Dreamtime there are myths of more recent times.

Maybe the most fascinating and undying modern legend out
here is that of Lasseter's Golden Reef. And as luck would have
it, a member of my own family was part of the story that
became legend. It's the story of a very public Outback expedition to find a huge deposit of gold that, legend had it, would
have been rich enough at the time to rescue the whole country
from the ravages of the Great Depression.

Harry Bell Lasseter claimed to have found a huge reef of
gold in a 7-mile-long outcrop of quartz west of Alice Springs

in 1897. He returned to it in 1899 and took geographical sight-
ings, but because of an error with his timepiece, his records
actually placed him, technically speaking, in the middle of the
Indian Ocean.

But Lasseter's recollections of the landmarks that he claimed
he could follow back to the gold were convincing enough to
become the focus of a new discovery expedition, which left
Alice Springs on 21 July 1930.

Hired as a bushman for his renowned local knowledge,
family legend has it, was my great grandfather Fred Nash
Colson. According to family diaries and stories passed on, Fred
had bush skills second to none in the Centre. At forty years of
age he was both strong enough to take on an arduous trip and
mature enough to have heard most of the tales and legends
passed on by settlers, who had first arrived in any numbers
sixty years before.

I have to tell you straight up that, judging from his diary,
Fred had his doubts about Lasseter from the word go. But these
blokes had a fair idea of where they wanted to go and Fred
knew the country they were heading for and could steer them
clear of more trouble.

So, hired to do a job – he was the only man on the expedition who wasn't a partner in whatever wealth they turned
up – Fred took it on for three pounds a day and set out to do
it to the best of his ability.

There are many books about the Lasseter legend – the
expeditions and the gold – and they all make for good reading.
If you could freeze the Loch Ness monster in one place, and
turn it into precious metal, I suppose you could say Lasseter's
Reef is Australia's Nessie. Everyone knows roughly where it
is, and there's no way it can be too far away from the tough

area everyone agrees is where it should be, but while many visitors and searchers have tried to lay hands on it, no one ever has.

And neither did Harry Bell Lasseter in 1931. In fact, since that year no one's ever laid hands on or seen hide nor hair of Lasseter, let alone his gold. One of the last people on earth who did see Lasseter and the camels he was riding west to his fabled fortune was Fred Colson.

As you can imagine, the family has lots of Lasseter stories in its collective storybook, but they all come to the same conclusion that Fred Colson did soon after meeting the man. Lasseter definitely was not a bushman, and was either a complete fake or had got himself into such secretive habits about protecting his lost gold, he couldn't separate truth from fiction himself any more. It was the same result for anyone putting faith in him, or, quite literally, going along for the ride: no gold, no millions of pounds in their or the country's coffers and, finally, no Lasseter.

Fred Colson's a legendary figure in Outback history, but should never be confused with his brother, Ted, who also contributed to the exploration and further knowledge of the local area. I don't use the word 'tamed', because even though Ted's achievement could be compared to that of better-known explorers who are said to have tamed a previously impenetrable area of the world, Ted never aimed to beat the land he lived in. Instead, he wanted to better understand its challenges and find a way to work within it.

The Simpson Desert is arid, being some of the toughest country on the continent. It spans about 145,000 square kilometres. Most of it is in the Territory, but it overlaps into Queensland and South Australia at the three cornered point where the borders of the two states and one territory meet. Its boundaries are marked on three sides by rivers: the Finke River in the west, the Mulligan and Diamantina Rivers to the east, and the Plenty River and the MacDonnell Ranges in the north (Plenty River is an ironic name for a river that runs through an area noted for punishing heat and the absence of water). It's southern boundary is closer to the nature of the Simpson – the normally dry, saline expanse of Lake Eyre.

The desert's terrain is characterised by sand dunes 20–37 metres high and 450 metres apart, which run parallel for up to 165 kilometres north-west to south-east across the desert. Spinifex grows between the dune crests, but not much else can stand it there. The desert is also the last refuge of some rare Australian desert animals, including the fat-tailed marsupial mouse.

All in all, it's a forbidding environment that had beaten every white man who ever tried to cross it west to east or back again. That is, until my great great uncle Ted became convinced the desert could be crossed and chose an exceptionally good season in which to do it. Maybe only during one two-month period of the year, and maybe waving goodbye to loved ones without a single guarantee he'd ever see them again, but Ted Colson thought it could be done and it was worth trying. Lucky for him his wife, Alice, agreed.

On the afternoon of 24 May 1936, with a string of five camels and in the company of an Aboriginal worker, Peter Aines, Ted Colson set out east for Birdsville from his station at Bloods Creek in northern South Australia.

Men had been into the Simpson before. There were 'tracks' laid out as far as the three-way meeting point of states and territory, which is known as Poeppel Corner. Augustus John

Poeppel had marked that point at 138 degrees longitude east with a post in 1879, and many others had reached it since, most on foot. Cecil Madigan famously flew over the desert in 1929 for an aerial survey that gave people the first complete 'picture' of the extent and challenge of the Simpson. He also pronounced it untravellable on ground level.

But Ted had already made his mind up that that wasn't so. Heading east he passed within 300 metres of Poeppel Corner and its marking post. He and Peter arrived in Birdsville after sixteen days crossing 400 kilometres of desert. They went to the pub, told people there where they'd just come from, and prepared to go straight back. The doubting Thomases were only silenced when Ted developed the photographs he'd taken along the way.

Doubts demolished, Ted and Peter kitted out their camels for the trip home to Bloods Creek. This time they actually walked right up to Poeppel's post, and took photographs of it.

Ted returned to his wife, Alice, who was very relieved to see him and then told him the woodpile needed refreshing.

The family history is dotted with men and women I can look back to for inspiration. But the achievements of my ancestors remind me more than anything else that humility needs to stay in pride of place in my kitbag. Because, whatever I achieve, it'll be part of a working and dreaming tradition that has kept the whole family going when we're up against and dealing with the big challenges.

We're still doing it today, as is every family taking breath on the face of this earth. I've learnt that nobody does it easy; all of us will be touched by disaster, by tragedy, by the results of our own rushes of blood, by the carelessness and unthinking cruelty of others.

What counts is not what you've done, but how what you've done might have helped others along the harder patches of the road we're all travelling. Fred Colson did it, Ted did too, my Dad's still doing it, Mum as well, all of us in our own ways. I could name a hundred names, people I know, doing the same. That's great, but what makes me feel even better is the knowledge that there are millions of people I will never know also helping those around them without any thought of reward or recognition.

Lasseter's gold might be still out there, but the real stuff is here, all around you every day. That's the secret Fred Colson passed down to us. It's a good one, I reckon. And I first learnt it at Waite River.

CHAPTER 3

··

GETTING A BROAD EDUCATION

When Dad and I had come back from that first bore run at Waite River, it sure seemed like our work had just begun.

'All work and no play ...' as the saying goes. Some wise old fella must have come up with that one, or maybe it was some cheeky young bloke. Either way, we had plenty of time to play at Waite River Station, so don't get the idea the land runs on child labour. It's simply that it's always a case of all hands on deck when there's a lot to be done. As it turns out, though, a lot of what on the face of it seems to be work is so much fun you find yourself volunteering to do it.

That might have had something to do with the fact that it wasn't soon after arriving at Waite River that we had to start going to school. Now, it wasn't *too* big a deal. No bus to catch, no bully in the playground trying to rub my face in the dirt, nobody else's school lunch I liked the look of better than mine.

Instead, school was in a room just off the kitchen in the staff quarters. We'd swing the radio aerial up over an old ironwood tree outside, now that it was clear of cats, and Simone and I (and Tanya, when she was old enough) would sit down near the old Codan radio run by battery and tune in to the School of the Air.

Most Outback kids were educated by correspondence and over the radio. Because, while Outback Australia is big enough to swallow up the twenty biggest states of the United States, for population density you might think you were on Mars.

It's communication technology that has bound the place together, from the first telegraph to the marvels of the Internet and satellite telephony.

But if anyone had to put their finger on the one form of communication that characterises the place, it'd be the ever-faithful if not 100 per cent reliable short-wave radio network. It seems like the radio's always been there, and if you had the ears to pick up every message being beamed out from every direction twenty-four hours a day, the last thing you could call the Red Centre is silent. Our lives are webbed together by radio.

People have had their lives saved by it, calling in the Flying Doctors. They've been married over it. Been caught out in slips of the tongue on it. Sold, bought and bartered over it. Cursed it, blessed it, been caught up in hot gossip over it, whispered into it and shouted at it.

And of course all we kids were educated over it.

I just wish no one had ever had the idea school should start before sunrise to get it over and done with before the real heat of the day set in. I would have much rather been out across the paddock at first light, which is the best part of the day, with that sun splashing fresh across the landscape, as old and spiritual as time itself.

Anyway, the law of the land did have that idea, so, like every other kid within range of the radio, I'd be up at six o'clock in the morning and start school by six-thirty or seven o'clock.

The truth of it is, you didn't spend too much time in front of the radio. Just enough for the school to make sure everyone was doing the same exercises and had had a chance to have a little chat with one another socially.

The hands-on heads-down work would go on between the governess and my sister and me. Governess? I hear you say. Well, they've always been a part of Outback life. Young women, maybe local, but just as likely from the city, or even overseas, who worked as teachers and general child carers when your mother was too busy running the property to be in six places at once, including the schoolroom. We had a few good governesses during our primary school years. Some would stay a year and others even longer.

The system seems to work for everybody. Many young women, most of them more adventurous than the average girl or they wouldn't be out here, work doing a job where that adventurousness is not only tested, it's more often than not rewarded with a whole new life.

Many of the women who now supervise fresh new governesses looking after station kids started out in the same role before meeting some bloke who had come mustering or was behind the wheel of a roadtrain from even a thousand miles away down the track, fell for him and married him. You'd be surprised at some of the accents you hear when the young mothers of central Australia get on the radio together or meet for special events.

Having a governess meant we could really focus on each lesson because the governess would only have two or three of us, not a classroom of forty kids demanding equal attention. This also meant school could be, in theory, over twenty times as fast. See, I must have been paying attention during my multiplication tables.

Fact is, I owe a lot of that to my Dad – again. There were a couple of points he was always very strong about. Doing the dishes was one. I'd do the dishes with my sisters, no nonsense about men's work and women's business, it was all shared work. And then we'd have to read particular times tables before we went to bed, which turned out really well because all through school I was okay at maths even if I was a bit slack about the rest of it.

With School of the Air you'd know your schoolmates through their voices and station call signs, but didn't see their faces until we all travelled hundreds of miles once a year for a get-together.

Admittedly, we were a touch crowded in at Waite River. Our nearest neighbours were all within 35 to 40 kilometres as the crow flies. There were the Webb family on Alcoota Station to the south, the Purvis family on Woodgreen to the west, and Utopia Station to the north.

We became friends with Shane and Sherrie Purvis from sharing 'desks' on the School of the Air, but we didn't actually meet for a while after exchanging radio call signs. It's a strange situation all Outback kids are familiar with.

But at the once-a-year get-togethers we would finally meet, often for the first time. The first get-together I ever went to was in the western MacDonnell Ranges, in a national park outside Alice Springs at a place called Simpson's Gap. At last

Simone and I met some of the kids we'd talked to over the two-way radio.

But the get-togethers weren't just ten minutes of 'Oh, so that's why they call you "Red"!' and then 'What do we do next?'. There would also be lots of activities, such as sports. Which was strange, because we never played sport or did many physical education classes, and we couldn't have team sports with a team spread over a million or so square kilometres.

But Outback kids are extremely active kids, and for sure I'd play with the local Aboriginal kids, so I could run and jump and put a bat on a ball or a stick on a paddy melon. Back then, it wasn't compulsory for some Aboriginal children to attend school, but get us School of the Air kids together for an organised sports meet, and you can imagine the chaos.

The spirit of the get-together would carry you through, with almost everyone going home with some small cup or ribbon. They were little things, but they bound us all together as a scattered community in many ways closer than some suburban cul-de-sacs ever become.

Apart from the sports activity, the school organised competitions like 'The Best Damper Maker' – things that kids were doing as part of everyday Outback life. I remember the time I came second in 'The Best Billy Tea' competition.

I was proud enough, out of a few kids, to come in second. But there's always been a real competitive streak in me, so, not too long after that I began to think that second was the first loser, which is an attitude that I take in most things I do.

But the trick is not to spit the dummy if someone else proves better on the day. Because there's always another day, and besides that, you never stop learning in this life. If there's anything somebody who's just beaten you can give you it's this – knowing how to make sure it doesn't happen again. You don't learn by getting mad about someone having the edge on you. You learn by spotting the edge and adding it to your own swag of skills.

At Waite River I was certainly filling up that swag, and not always in the schoolroom. In some ways, it was too bad I never had a mechanic as a governess, because from a very early age I'd race away from the schoolroom to the big shed, and get down to trying to fix some engine or generator that was faulty, or mend any flat tyres. I had to know why things worked. It's all very well to flick a switch, turn a key, shift a gear and have something happen, but I always wanted to know *why*.

I'd go out on my scavenging trips, picking up bits and pieces from all around the house and down the Aborigines' camp.

Mum once told me I'd made the shed look like Steptoe & Son had set up shop Down Under. By the time she was half through explaining that one to me, I was just as seriously explaining as only a seven year old can do that my treasures were not junk. No way.

At one stage I set up shop as local mechanic for the Aborigines and the odd traveller who came through with a missing fan belt, flat tyre, knocking sound under the bonnet, smoke pouring out of the exhaust or no electricity to the distributor. But I'd get frustrated if I couldn't fix something or couldn't work out what the problem was.

I sure learnt a thing or two from some of the Aboriginal boys. They'd had times when they were stuck on the road for days on end, with no choice but to improvise and fix their car somehow. If a vehicle is on its last legs and you need to get that last 20 kilometres out of it there's no doubt in my mind you need an Aboriginal bush mechanic!

I was like any normal kid wanting to play or go on an adventure but when I wasn't alone in the big old shed struggling with a set of points or a seized-up old pump, I tried to muck in and make Mum's life a little easier.

Of course, to get things done out here you need to get around. One thing Dad was determined we kids should be able to do early was drive. You never know when the only person around after an accident or something that's put an adult out of commission miles from anywhere could be a kid. So, there I was, all of six years old, when Dad propped me up behind the wheel of the old four-wheel-drive. He showed me the pedals then told me to put my foot on the clutch. Stretching down to reach it I disappeared between the seat and the steering wheel.

Even so, I could just peer through the wheel over the dashboard to see where I was going. A couple of trials up and back the short drive and a few kangaroo hops and stalls later, I was getting the hang of the gears and the coordination of it all.

Now, it just so happened that the vehicle had on the back of it about 800 kilos of cement and sheets of iron to build a new tank. Dad reckoned I should drive through the main gate. So I'd driven 5 kilometres out from the house and was heading home, feeling like I was some sort of natural behind the wheel, when up looms the gate.

I changed down a gear, reckoned I'd lined the truck up dead centre, headed straight on through, and *crrr-runchhh*!

I'd misjudged it by the half a metre or so hanging out the side of the tray, and had hooked a corner of the gate on the left-hand side and dragged the whole load off the back. It all hit the ground, every bit of it.

Dad shook his head, but he always saw the funny side of things. We spent the next hour putting all the stuff back on, then he made me drive the rest of the way home. I reckon he figured that if you fall off a horse you get straight back on.

After that I used to drive around the station whenever I got the chance, driving an old Suzuki that took me just about everywhere four wheels could go and come back from. I always stuck to the roads because Dad was never happy about people driving off the beaten track if it wasn't necessary, as it harms the environment.

The driving came in handy for all sorts of things. When I was about nine or ten I set up business. I'd collect all the scrap metal, aluminium, copper and all that retrievable stuff from the rubbish dumps of the station. I'd also get old batteries and radiators from old wrecks in the Aborigines' camps. I'd go along there in the little Suzuki, pull up beside a car that's just been sitting out in the weather for years with the engine already out of it and get my spanners out and go to work. I'd pull the radiator out, as well as any wire cables that were there and anything with copper. I'd strip the cables with my pocket knife and put them all in the big 44-gallon drum in the back, which pretty soon would be full of scrap metal.

Then, whenever Dad or someone was going to town, I'd chuck the drum in the back of Mum's old twin-cab Dyna truck, rope it on the back, and off we'd go. By the time I was ten years old I had about ninety-eight dollars in the bank.

I'd built that total up with regular visits to the local police station, too. We used to have lots of dingoes around the place, which would cause more trouble than they were worth, especially when they were interbreeding with the Aborigines' camp dogs, and attacking new-born calves.

The station hands would cull them and I'd take their scalps and hang them out to dry in the rafters of the old tractor shed. Once dried out they'd go into an old hessian bag ready to be taken in to the local police station, were they'd give me two dollars' bounty a head, because they were officially vermin, a real stock killer.

I did quite well out of selling scalps, and at the time I thought I was just about set for life.

But money doesn't set you up, knowledge does. And while I liked the School of the Air, the best school I've ever been to is the Outback. I've learnt more about animals and plants and people and the world there than I've learnt just about anywhere else. It's just a pity that all Australian kids can't attend it!

CHAPTER 4

···

OLD MOSE AND OTHER WAITE RIVER INHABITANTS

The tempo had sure picked up at Waite River when my Dad started setting the pace. But the people who stayed working with us were happy to see Waite River get back into productive top gear.

They were all real characters, as most people are in the bush, but the blokes who stick in my mind most are Ray Mosely, Bill Collins, Graham Martin and David Handley, our main group of stockmen.

Only one of them, usually Old Mose, would stay on the station while the others went out on the musters with Dad. But when they were all back on the station, the place had a real busy feel to it.

The other mob who made Waite River what it was, and helped shape the special memories it holds for me, were the Aborigines working and living there. There was the Bird family: Colin, who became one of my closest childhood friends, Tommy, Joe, Mavis, Hilda, June – the list goes on, as there were around thirty of them living there, and the names come back with grins and good times attached.

I learnt so much about the country all around – what was in it and under it – from those local people. If the School of the Air was all about white fella's learning – the three Rs and who put what flags where – the school of the 'there' was where my Aboriginal friends taught me how to survive and to hopefully be the sort of human being you could trust. There are no walls where they live: as far as you can see, to the left and right of the horizon is a temporary wall. The roof, well, that's the lights of the Southern Cross.

When Dad was away I'd go out with Mose – Ray Mosely – to look after the bores around the place. Mose was a little younger than Dad. Part Aboriginal, he stood only about five foot five, but he had a big heart.

He was a bit of a joker, too. Once, Ray and I were going out on a serious job, doing a bore run like the one I'd done with Dad. We made a good team. I'd open and shut the gates for him, and he'd let me drive the old truck every so often. Driving the truck was the highlight of my life. But, you know, even the most exciting things can get a little routine, so this time I decided to spice things up a bit.

We'd had a bit of lightning and thunder, a bit of rain with it too, but we drove along, dodging the puddles, and I was having the time of my life. Finally we got to Muller Bore. Everything looked ship-shape, but we had to start the motor as the tank was only half full. The old Southern Cross motor was inside a corrugated iron shed that the wind must've been holding up, it looked so rickety. Ray got out of the truck and walked over to the shed.

'See you later, Mose,' I said. Then I drove off, for a couple of kilometres, probably, laughing myself silly thinking that it was the best trick I'd ever pulled.

Finally, I turned around and I went back to the shed. Mose was back there waiting, looking cool as you like, smoking a Log Cabin rollie. I pulled up, had a bit of a laugh and said, 'All right, mate, what's happening?'

Well, Old Mose had a poker face on him, just like every other day of his life, but he knew me better than I thought, what with me and machinery and everything.

'Oh,' he said. 'Why don't you just go in that shed, see if you want to try and start that motor.'

'Beauty,' I thought. See, you have to give a fairly big crank to those motors. You have to crank them over with the decompression lever down to turn them, and once you've got enough speed you have to release the lever, being careful the compression doesn't break a young arm doing it. Dad had told me to wait another year till I had more strength before I tried it.

Well, right or wrong, I wanted to try it now. Mose leant back on the truck and watched me go inside. I got on with checking the oil and water. I was feeling pretty proud of myself, because every time I looked up there was Old Mose nodding at me as if to say, 'Good, that's right, well done Troy.'

I went to start the motor up and after a couple of attempts I surprised myself and got it going. It was making a hell of a racket in the old tin shed: the world could've fallen in and I wouldn't have heard it. I know that for sure, because I didn't hear Mose start up the truck and drive away.

When I walked outside with a cool step in my stride, he was a hundred metres away, waving back at me: 'Go-o-od-b-y-y-ye!!'

Right then the heavens opened up and rain poured down. I raced back into the shed. Before I knew it, half the local wildlife was trying to get into the dry with me. Or at least it seemed that way. A centipede came flying across the entrance and a scorpion right after it. I thought I'd been left out there on my own, and every monster was coming bubbling up out of my worst nightmare. I was stamping on these things before they got me, and looking outside seeing nothing but rain, a curtain of the stuff, with no Mose anywhere. A large bolt of lightning sent me back deep into that shed.

At last the rain stopped, and still no Mose. I started to get worried he'd gone and left me all the way out there – you know, got his revenge big time. It was not much more than half an hour all up before he came back, but it seemed like hours.

He'd obviously just gone out a little way to check the holding paddock, probably not even thinking about getting back at me, for all I know. But right at that moment it wasn't only the ground drying round the shed that was steaming as he drove up.

I bit my tongue the whole way home, just grunting at Mose as he pointed stuff out I'd have been up on my toes to get a look at any other time. But when he pulled up outside the house, I was out of that truck and straight in to see Mum.

'Mose is sacked,' I said. Before she could get a word in, I told her he could pack his bags, grab his swag, whistle to his dog, and leave the station at an old jig jog.

I must've looked like thunder on a stick, because Mum broke out laughing before I was halfway through why Mose should have his notice. She got out of me the joke I'd played on him first and said something like 'Teach an old dog new tricks and it just might turn around and bite you.' But all I could see was that Mose was working for us, Mum and Dad and everyone, and he hadn't pulled his weight so his job was on the line.

Of course, I was just an eight-year-old kid acting too big for the wrong pair of boots. Mose was actually worth his weight in gold, otherwise Dad wouldn't have felt confident leaving him to keep an eye on things while he was away.

❖　❖　❖

Mose could turn his hand to most things, and he did. Once he went over to another property called Kianina where he was taking delivery of some cattle, with the manager, my uncle Albie Colson.

We kids were all there with Mose, camping outside with our sleeping swags up off the ground on cyclone beds.

Come daybreak, we woke and that swag wasn't flat out any more. It was galloping around like a sack with epilepsy. It's the only swag I've ever seen tearing up and down the Outback, but Mose was such a joker we figured he was putting on a wake-up show for all of us.

Not so. Because Mose, who prided himself on his independence, had not woken alone, but his sleeping companion was no man's ideal mate. Mose had opened his eyes and felt something at the bottom of his swag, lovingly curled around his feet. Mose knew what a snake felt like. What he didn't know was what sort of snake had crept into his swag, but he wasn't waiting to find out. Instead, he'd tried to slip out of the swag. But the snake woke up.

More in than out, Mose was up on those feet and running for it, but he didn't get far all wrapped up in the swag. The snake was mad now, and it bit him a few times.

Mose was squirming and bellowing like a bull. He finally got himself out, and right after him came a 1-metre-long king brown snake. The thing shot off.

Mose stood there making his peace with the world, although, from what was coming out of his mouth, he still had a few scores to settle.

We got him to the Alice Springs hospital in record time, and Mose came through, tough as nails, lucky for him.

The next thing that came through was a brand new cyclone bed from town, marked 'Hand Deliver Ray Mosely'. Sure, Mose could do most things, but I never knew him to be a boilermaker. Still, the first thing he did when he got that bed was have the steel legs extended.

I don't want you to get the idea that you can't put a foot down out here without stepping on something venomous. But sometimes it just seemed that, for all the great wide space out here, trouble had a way of finding us.

And king browns can be trouble. One targeted another good stockman, Graham, who was about seventeen years old. Graham could ride a horse, ride motor bikes and seemed pretty smooth at everything he turned his hand to, and I used to think that I wanted to be as good a ringer as he was.

After school one morning, I was out the front of the house when I heard the bike. It was sort of screaming, with really high revs, the way someone might ride who didn't really know what they were doing, pushing the machine but not getting the best out of it.

I looked down to the front gate between the two sheds. It was Graham. He'd pulled up at the gate and thrown it open. Then he pushed it shut without chaining it, which was not like him, no way. But he gunned away again and came flying towards the sheds. I knew something had to be wrong, so I ran up to the sheds just as he pulled up. He just fell right off the bike and lay on the ground, yelling, 'Snake bite. A brown. Snake got me.'

He'd been bitten on the foot. I ran into the house to get Mum, and she got straight on the radio to the Flying Doctor. The nearest place they could get to a good runway in time was Utopia Station, about 30 kilometres away.

Mum and the governess got Graham's boot off, and I got a close look at the bite.

He'd had on a brand new pair of R.M. Williams riding boots, tough as they get, but when I held his boot up to the sky it was just like someone had drilled two holes through the top of it. Even now I find it hard to believe that a snake's fangs could pierce leather like that, but when we got the story out of Graham after he came home, I for one could understand just how mad that snake must've been. If I'd had my wits about me, or, at least, my nose, I might have recognised the smell of barbecued snake, but that just wasn't grabbing my attention at the time.

Apparently, Graham had been out riding a fence run, looking for any breaks in the wire or posts coming loose. He'd ridden down a bit of a gully, or gilgai, which is natural erosion formed by the contours of the land, and he'd changed down to third gear or so on the way. When he reached the bottom, right there in front of his bike – too close to miss, and no way was he about to stop – was a huge king brown. Graham changed down to second to speed out of there but, as he drove over the king brown, it threw itself up around the exhaust of the motor bike.

Not something any living thing would want to cuddle,

especially one with a belly full of poison it's mad enough to be happy enough to share around. The snake burnt and singed itself like crazy, and part of it was getting beaten around by the rear wheel, as well. Its head must have just swung around as Graham's foot moved to change gear to get enough power to come back up the other side of the gilgai. That movement was enough for the maddest snake for a million miles.

Snap! It struck his foot and bit right through the leather. Graham's boot actually saved his life, because the venom stayed on the outside of it. Only a relatively small amount of venom was injected into the top of Graham's foot, but it was enough to put him in hospital for a week.

This set a few hearts racing round the district. Graham was a good-looking bloke, and when the word got out that he was lucky to be alive, a few of the local girls brought forward plans they'd been hatching for him. Sure enough, thanks to R.M. Williams and a mad-as-hell king brown, Outback Australia had one less bachelor not long after.

To my nine-year-old mind, that was the least interesting part of the whole story. I was quite sure that the snake must've been the same one I saw that first day when I rode the main gate into Waite River. The block was a bit of a haven for those snakes, but, who knows, it might have been the same old snake. Fact is, if a king brown bites you, it doesn't matter too much whether you've actually met before. They're one and all deadly, whatever basis of familiarity you may be on.

❖ ❖ ❖

Snakes and lizards, insects, birds, flora – as soon as you start looking closely at the unforgiving environment of my favourite place on earth and know what you're looking for you find it's teeming with living things.

And you can bet there's an Aboriginal name for everything that's ever set down roots, flown above, bounded through, slithered across or burrowed under this wide red land.

I have a fair idea of that because so much of my youth was spent with Aborigines – kids and adults – who, through everyday play and the important activities of hunting and food foraging, showed me the 'hidden' treasures of Outback Australia. Creatures, water where there appears none to drink, and edible plants where the landscape seems empty of anything more sustaining than scrappy scrub and spindly trees.

I used to spend as much time as possible out exploring the Waite River block with Colin and other Aboriginal kids, and we'd all go out hunting together. Not too many of them could shoot so straight, and I can tell you from experience, as good as spears and throwing sticks are at hunting game, you can come back in with a weary arm and not much to show for it using traditional weapons. As I'd learnt to shoot my slug gun, Colin would ask me to use his .22-calibre rifle to get kangaroos for his family.

Among the many other protein-rich creatures that we hunted and cooked on hot coals were goannas. They've traditionally been a valuable food source during periods of drought when kangaroos, wallabies and emus are hard to find.

I can only talk about my own part of the world, because Aborigines roamed far and wide over the entire continent, but in central Australia the locals have identified more than 140 species of flora and fauna as food. That's the sort of range and variety modern supermarket managers are happy to have on their shelves.

Of course, in recent times Aborigines haven't had to rely solely on the bush for their tucker. Most stations have a store where they can buy flour and sugar, jam, tinned fruit as well as other things you can truck in from town to make the diet a little more interesting than foraged and hunted bush food.

At Waite River Mum had fixed up the old saddle shed as the store and set opening hours on Mondays and Fridays only, so that she didn't have to spend every odd minute of the day running it when someone came knocking on the door.

But while all those supplies are pretty necessary, many Aborigines still live as close as they can to the traditional life-style, including what they eat. And what they traditionally eat is bush tucker. Usually it's the men who hunt the game, but in my experience it's the women who provide for the table more than the men. Their every-day job is to search out the seasonal bush fruits and vegetables that are so rich in vitamins, to support the protein of the meat the men bring in.

The women also dig up tubers and delicacies such as witch-etty grubs and honey ants with digging sticks, collecting fruit and seeds in the wooden containers they carry. Both men and women hunt lizards and small marsupials, the children usually along with the women. As boys reach puberty they start to spend most of their time with the mature males, learning how to be men.

In a traditional tribal situation, hunters, the elders, initiators, pregnant women and children are each allocated certain parts of the animal, and the remainder is shared among the other members of the family groups. Seeds are ground and mixed with water to make a nutritious paste that's cooked in the coals, as well.

The thing I could never get used to was the way they'd eat

their meat: not medium-rare but rare-rare, still blood red! But the meat didn't last too long after the kill before being eaten, so bacteria never really got a chance to breed.

The game is lower in fat and cholesterol than the domesticated animals being eaten by the family and me in Waite River's dining room. And I knew that the bush fruits and vegetables provided plentiful vitamins. But, much as I enjoyed it, I could never go past Mum's cooking.

Being an adventurous boy, it mightn't have seemed the best part of those days back then, but what I learnt about the plants, the fruit and vegetables of the Outback has proved the most important legacy. The wild berries, bananas, the bush pineapples, coconuts, oranges – you name it – the bush fruit have all proved to be real lifesavers. Not knowing what I was looking at could have seen the harsh conditions of the Outback claim another victim of ignorance.

But hunting bush tucker has its own dangers. I remember a story Mose told me once, about how it can actually get you killed. Or near enough. He swears it's true, and I have no reason to doubt him any more than he does me, when yarns are spinning round the late-night campfire.

Mose reckons he and a couple of Aboriginal women were driving a ute over a big claypan flat with a couple of other blokes in the back. There wasn't a tree in sight: it was like Mars in tourist brochures. Then they saw a big perenty, a goanna that is Australia's largest lizard. It was close to 2 metres long, beautiful, covered in yellow spots of various shades and markings. But perenties are also a bit of a delicacy with the Aborigines – they just love them for their really sweet meat.

Quick as lightning, this old mate leapt off the back of the ute and started running after the lizard with his spear. Well, the perenty had other ideas than making this bloke's belly bend out a bit, so he led him a merry chase.

Mose and the others in the ute were laughing like mad, tears running down their faces, because they reckoned this old chilpy had always been a bit lazy. He'd never lifted a finger he hadn't had to – but he loved perenty cooked just right.

The old fella ran himself ragged pretty quickly, so he stopped where he was, panting like mad, and leant on his spear. His wife, paralysed by the shock of seeing the old bloke move faster than she can remember him ever doing, realised things were back where they usually were – she was going to have to do all the work. So she jumped out of the ute with a big flat shovel in one hand.

Soon she was running around chasing the perenty, smashing down the shovel, trying to wallop it, but missing every time. The lizard must have decided it'd had enough, so it looked around for a tree to shoot up, away from these crazies with their spears and shovels.

Mose reckons the perenty must have figured the old mate out there standing with his spear catching his breath looked a bit like a tree. So he just scuttled across the flat and ran straight up the side of the old Aborigine and sat on top of his head.

The bloke was too stunned to do anything but just stand there with this big overgrown goanna on his head, all 2 metres of him, his tail hanging down the old bloke's back, with his claws digging into his scalp.

The old girl saw this, but what she really saw was dinner, or maybe she saw a chance to get back at the old bloke for twenty or thirty years of never lifting a finger. Who knows, but she ran up to him and 'Whack!', down came the shovel on the perenty on this bloke's head.

The problem was, the lizard was thinking faster than anyone else out there. He was long gone by the time the shovel made contact; he'd jumped clear off the old bloke's head, hit the ground running and clean escaped.

The old chilpy stood there for a second, and then fell flat over. His wife didn't even notice: she took off after the lizard. But he was seeing daylight as sure as the old bloke was seeing stars, and the woman couldn't get to him.

Finally she came back to the ute. Mose had the old bloke, head split, lying out in the back, sore and sorry. They drove home, the two hunters arguing like mad, until the old bloke just wrapped his big old shirt around his head, so he couldn't see or hear anything.

And that's when Mose reckons he saw the old fella's wife crack a grin as wide as the whole Outback.

It's lucky the Outback's so big. Because I can tell you now, the people in it are larger than life.

CHAPTER 5

LICORICE AND POWDERPUFF

There are a lot more animals out here than people, and you get to know them pretty well.

At Waite River, cats weren't the only trouble makers on the block. The Isaacsons had also left us a small herd of goats. Thinking back, I'm not sure who really owned Waite River before our family arrived, because the goats had the run of the place, too. They'd eat anything they could get to, and could do a clean sweep of the overgrown garden if you let them. Even the clothes Mum hung on the washing line weren't safe if you left the gate open.

Those goats would get themselves into the tightest corners. Like the outside dunny, for example. On one occasion, Mum and we kids came back from town to find that a nanny goat and two wethers had somehow got in there and had closed the door behind them. They were bleating and butting at the door – they hadn't done themselves any harm – but I reckon if they'd thought things through, they'd have played to their strength and eaten their way out.

And of course, there were the dogs that lived around the Aborigines' camp. We saw more of them than the stock we wanted to see, even though we culled them to minimise long-term damage.

But the animals that go hoof in hand with people working the land out here are horses. Most of us are in a saddle before we can walk away from the beast wearing it.

At Waite River I mainly rode two horses: Licorice and PowderPuff.

Back then, I might have been little but Licorice wasn't much bigger. He was a black Shetland pony about 3 feet tall. But it's not size that matters, it's the attitude packaged in there, and anyone can tell you that, sweet as a little pocket horse like Shetlands might look, they can be the most contrary creatures in the whole equine family.

With Licorice as my partner, I thought I could be the Cisco Kid. We didn't get to see TV much, without one on the station or the signal to reach us out there, but when we went into town – which was half a dozen times a year – I was always glued to Grandma's set watching 'The Cisco Kid'. I pestered and pestered Mum and Dad till they got me the Cisco kit – the chaps, the big Mexican cowboy hat, the silver guns, the whole pocket-Cisco look.

On my birthday, I had a few of my friends over. With an audience to watch me in my whole Cisco get-up, I jumped on Licorice shouting to everyone, 'Hey, look at this. Look here. I'm the Cisco Kid!', as I fired my cap guns, *bang, bang*.

Whoever I thought I was, Licorice knew who he was. And

he was the bloke who didn't want anyone on his back. He thought, 'I'll give *you* bang, bang alright, young Troy.' He put in a few pigroots and hurled me sky-high. Well, sky-high as a Shetland can hurl anyone, but it's always a long way down the moment you hit the dirt. Not the coolest Cisco Kid that ever was.

Licorice certainly had a mind of his own. He might have been only 3 feet tall, but I'm sure he thought he was a wild brumby stallion. When he was out in a big paddock with other horses, big as they might be, he'd gallop two steps to their one, always leading the way, flat out thinking he was a leader.

When the others had to stop at a fence, Licorice's party trick was to go right under. Tanya was riding him once, when she was about six years old. They were coming along behind a mob of cattle we were bringing up, when a bullock clean broke away. She kicked little Licorice after him like she'd been in the ringer's seat for years.

My sisters are great riders and Tanya's no exception: she wheeled the beast around and back toward the mob. But the bullock went straight past the mob and straight under the fence. Unfortunately, so did Licorice.

Small as she was, Tanya couldn't make herself smaller as the little pony went straight under the barbed wire. Luckily, Dad came to the rescue and reefed her off Licorice before there was too much damage, although she still wears the barbed wire scars today.

And Licorice? He must've figured all the Dann kids could use a lesson in which end of the reins you'd find the boss.

Kids were still learning to ride on him when I had graduated to full-size mounts. And learning a lot quicker than they thought they might have to how to come off, too. They say you have to come off at least seven times before you can ride okay. Well, I truly passed that in my childhood!

❖   ❖   ❖

My first real horse was PowderPuff. He'd been named before I met him – by a practical joker, I reckon. PowderPuff was a strawberry roan pony, not a big bloke, only about fourteen and a half hands, but with a personality as huge as any four-legged creature I've ever met. Bigger than some on two legs, for that matter.

Whenever a ringer or a stockman would try to get on him at the station he would leave them on their backsides if they weren't quick enough to mount. Somehow, the two of us had a bond, though. I'd like to think it was based on mutual respect, but thinking back it might have been something else on PowderPuff's part. Patience, perhaps, or sheer disbelief. People used to laugh at the way I'd climb up his leg. I'd literally wrap my hands around his leg and climb up like a fireman going up a pole. I'd grab the pommel of the saddle, put my knee in the stirrup, and then pull myself up into the saddle.

PowderPuff would turn his head and watch me doing this, and I wouldn't look in his eyes, because I knew he was think-ing, 'What the hell is this little bloke trying to do?' But he always stood and waited until I was in the saddle, pleased as Punch with myself, as my parents and everyone laughed about it.

I must've looked like a crab crawling over a rock. But that's the point. PowderPuff wouldn't stand still for big blokes who could almost step into his saddle, but he put up with me. I reckon PowderPuff, the terror of the mounting yard, was just struck dumb, stony-still amazed as I clambered up on to him.

PowderPuff wouldn't let anyone on him but me; Licorice had had enough before my feet were in the stirrups. Just as well it wasn't the other way round, because it was PowderPuff who had to carry me in events at gymkhanas, race meetings and rodeos. It was very hard for us to win an event because I'd always be competing with kids older than I was, but I got the odd ribbon here and there.

From all the events I competed in over ten years or so, I reckon I won around fifty ribbons: a few firsts, lots of seconds, and thirds and stuff like that. They really test the skills you need to keep sharp. But the days I think of as the best, the ribbons that have pride of place, I won as a youngster on old PowderPuff. He was a top horse.

He would have been about twenty-five or twenty-six years of age when he passed away. That's a lot of my life.

It was a lot of my life, but not all of it was work and competition. PowderPuff and I would go out on our own, just exploring the beauty of the surrounding country. When there was good ground water, we'd ride through really wide creeks lined with beautiful trees, red gums and ghost gums along banks that six months before (and six months ahead), might have been 20 or 30 metres from even a sniff of running water. Those great old trees were just amazing.

But not everything is exactly what your eyes tell you, either because you aren't looking right or because you don't have the eyes to see. Life's always got a lesson coming up, and how many of them come out of nowhere?

On one particular day, I was riding with Simone and Penny, who was our governess at the time. I pulled up by a tree to tighten the girth on my saddle. The girls were doing a bit of circle work in a dry creek bed, so I decided to sit at the base of a ghost gum where the roots showed above the ground, holding the reins loosely in my hands.

I didn't look too closely – just sat straight down in a patch of shade. It must have been only a second, maybe even one of those split ones, before I'd been bitten by three or four inch ants. The experts reckon seven bites can kill you. I can tell you one bite doesn't give you any pleasure, and three you're already thinking way past seven.

I let out a few bellows and startled poor old PowderPuff. When I took off at a flat bolt, reins tight in my fist now, he tried to keep up with me at a gallop, and then, with all my yelping, he was past me, pulling away sidewards at the same time. I was going the other way because, at that stage of my life, if something hurt me I just wouldn't stand still – I'd have to start running around in circles.

The girls must have thought I'd finally flipped out, and troppo season wasn't even on us yet. It comes early to some, they probably thought when they looked over at me. They finally settled us both down and I took them back to the tree to show them what had happened.

After they'd got that much sense out of me, they took a peek at the bites, which were already as big as golf balls, making my backside hurt even more.

We all got home, me not walking with much of a swagger in my step as we went in.

The old inch ants had taught me about the poison they've got in their nippers. Since you've learnt that lesson by reading it here, you've done a whole lot better than I did.

I couldn't blame PowderPuff in a situation like that. There's not a lot that makes sense to a horse other than danger, a good feed, fresh water and a chance to stretch your legs. Throw in strange, yelling behaviour from the little two-legged types, and is it any wonder a horse decides, 'Let me outta here.'?

Another day I'd saddled up PowderPuff to go out mustering with Dad. I was crossing the Muller Creek, a really beautiful creek, with big red gums along the bank. So beautiful you'd never pick it for a death trap. I was guiding PowderPuff through a damp patch when all of a sudden he sort of half-staggered. He was up to his knees in quicksand.

I hardly had time to think before the stuff had stopped him dead in his tracks with me on top adding extra weight to the problem. I was really spooked and worried, especially for PowderPuff, so I jumped off his back, luckily clearing the few feet of quicksand and landing near the bank. PowderPuff was struggling, probably driving himself deeper by trying to get out, just as Dad and a couple of boys turned up. They all pitched in and helped him out. Saved, he just stood on the bank shaking big clumps of sand off him. Then I'm sure he winked at me, saying he was okay, because PowderPuff was my best mate in those days.

Another time, Dad wanted to muster a big paddock, so he got me to go and get the horses in out of the horse paddock. PowderPuff and I went out into pebbly, hilly country with gully flats in between, a mixture of red and limestone soils supporting gidgee trees, whitewoods, supplejacks, ironwoods and witchetty bushes. I brought in the horses that Dad was after, got them all into the yard, feeling proud and thinking about what Mum had made for dinner, when a young colt shot straight past me and out the gate.

I quickly shut the gate on the rest of the mob, jumped back on PowderPuff, who was not so happy about this turn of events, and kicked him after the young stallion, already a good half kilometre away and still galloping.

Whatever PowderPuff might've felt about doing overtime, he knew a challenge when he thought he saw it. So he just let rip after the other horse, galloping through a patch of woolly oat grass. There was a big log half hidden in the grass and he launched himself over it. I hadn't even seen the log, and I came out of the saddle, it took me so much by surprise. I had desert boots on, because the heel had broken on my riding boots, so, sure enough, my backside was in mid-air but my foot had slipped straight through the stirrup. I came off, but my foot was caught, and I was dragged by one foot at the heels of a racing PowderPuff.

And he was racing all right, now that he no longer was carrying my weight. I was alongside him for about 30 metres, just bouncing along the ground, most of my shirt torn off, cuts on my back, gravel rash, and a view of the world passing by I never want to see again. Then he reached the creek.

PowderPuff jumped it, and luckily my foot slid through the stirrup, leaving me sore and sorry in the creek as he galloped off.

I picked myself up, glad at least that that didn't mean I had to go looking for any bits that had come off, and I shuffled back to the homestead.

I never ended up getting that colt, because he was too smart and he'd had the wind under his heels from the instant he took his chances at that gate. Later in life I was to learn that this particular stallion would always try and pull the wool over someone's eyes, because a spoilt animal that's had a win is harder to educate than a wild one. And the funny thing is he was both!

The other thing I learnt a lesson about was the boots. As

Mum explained to me: 'That's why you wear your riding boots, Troy – not your desert boots – then your foot can't slip through the stirrup for a start, and when you're in an emergency, your riding boot will slip out relatively easily. You want to thank your lucky stars you didn't come off a lot worse for wear.'

Point taken, I went back out into the paddock and caught up with old PowderPuff. He'd thrown in the towel, too, but he pretended he'd been out there getting spelled for a month or two. So he gave me a deadpan look like, 'Long time, no see, young Troy.' The saddle he was still wearing undercut that little act.

I patted his neck, knowing full well it wasn't his fault but mine, and led him back in over the same ground I'd just done a 30-kilometres-an-hour sweep across. But this time we were agreed: we'd take it a bit more slowly. We weren't in any hurry.

That's called teamwork, and horses are important members of the team out here.

CHAPTER 6

....

BUMPS, SCRAPES AND CHRISTMAS DAY

Sometimes I would jump out of bed in the morning thankful I still had legs to stand on and arms to buzz off the lazy flies that breed in the green grass of a good Outback season.

Bumps and scrapes went round the whole family, from Simone breaking her arm playing cricket at school to mishaps closer to home.

I've probably broken or bent more bones on bikes than I like to think back over (Mum hates them), but the first real dust-up could just as easily have been the last.

It happened on Christmas Day, which is always a special event, with relatives coming from all directions. When you live in the middle of the country, people travel a long way to share some Christmas cheer.

Mum and Dad felt a traditional Christmas brought the whole station together. In that spirit, one year, Dad took us kids out to find the perfect Christmas tree. We took just one branch off a big bush pine near North Bore on a ridge. Standing on its end the branch was big enough to pass for a tree in itself, but the rest of the tree was still alive to provide Christmas trees for years to come.

On Christmas morning Dad would tell us he'd seen signs that Father Christmas had been through the night before. We tracked him right around the place, Dad, Simone, Tanya and I, moving through the close-in sheds, around the yards, stopping off at the chicken shed, saying 'Happy Christmas!' to the goats, and all the time pointing out the little hints and signs that the old bloke had left on his way to the house. You see, in the Outback, Father Christmas has his sled pulled by six big red kangaroos. True story.

The final evidence was there all right: kangaroo footprints. Santa Claus had left the whole family a swag of presents, and when Dad opened the fridge he showed me that old Father Christmas had collected his presents, too. The two cans of beer we'd put in there last night were gone, keeping the happy old bloke just a little happier as he ranged around the many stations that were waiting on him just as we'd been.

But I have mixed memories of 25 December at Waite River: amazement and wonder, as a child, at the thought that Father Christmas had been to visit, but also my first real experience of physical pain.

On this particular Christmas day, Auntie Fran and Uncle Bert had come out from Alice Springs to our place for a big roast dinner.

It was still early Christmas morning and Simone and my cousin Lisa had sneaked off to try these things called cigarettes. They'd gone a couple of kilometres from the homestead.

I jumped on the Honda XR75 motor bike to chase after them. My cousin Steven, on the 185 motor bike (which to us then was a big bike) was a minute behind me as I gunned away from the house.

I reached the point where the girls had turned off the road, but there was a big windrow there. Rocks and soil and trees had been pushed off the road so I couldn't cross it. I looked over my shoulder back down the road and I could see my cousin Steve about 500 metres away. I figured he was safely far enough away, so I just went up a little bit further and turned to cross the road.

But Steve had actually gunned the motorbike to catch up just after I'd spotted him. He must've been sitting on about 120 or 130 kilometres an hour and, as I turned, he ran straight into me. He missed my leg by a whisker or I wouldn't have one there today. But he hit everything else.

I was hurled off the bike and knocked unconscious. The girls came running over then raced back to the homestead, and Dad and Uncle Bert picked Steve and me up in the car, as Steve had a broken arm.

An ambulance had to come from Alice Springs, so Dad organised to meet it halfway. I came to, but I was concussed. The way the story's told, I went around thanking everyone: all my relatives, everyone there, giving Mum a big hug and kiss, thanking her for giving me a good life and looking after me. I apologised: 'Sorry I have to go now,' because, of course, I thought I was dying. I shook my uncle's hand then shook Dad's hand and said, 'Nice knowing you, mate. Take care of yourself and look after the family, and let everyone know I loved them! We might catch up one day somewhere.'

The women were upset, but they got me to the ambulance

where they gave me some morphine. When I woke up I was arriving at the hospital. I remember it well, because all I had for Christmas dinner was a mongrel old ham sandwich with bread that must have been a week old. I'd traded Christmas dinner for a broken collarbone and a fractured ankle when a moment of bike-riding inexperience caught up with me.

But just about the first thing I did when I got home was fix up the bike and head right out again.

❖   ❖   ❖

Another Christmas also had its thrills and spills, and they all started with a deal Simone and I did with Dad to skip washing the mountain of dishes that had piled up from Christmas dinner. Dad told us that if Simone and I went out and got the cow in ready for milking the next morning we could get out of doing the dishes.

I thought this was the best idea I'd heard for a long time. We'd get this milking done, no problems at all, we'd done it enough before.

We had an old Jersey cow out in the house paddock, which was about a square kilometre in size. She'd put herself right out in the middle of the paddock with her young calf alongside her.

A cow gets very protective of her calf, and this cow was also cranky by nature.

Simone had had a run-in the day before with this cow, so she just hung on the gate, too frightened to come in. But I'll be all right, I thought, so I walked out there about 200 metres. The calf ran of, so I chased after it to push it back to the mother so I could get them both into the yard. Of course, all the cow saw was me chasing her calf, so she thundered up and hit me at full pelt. I was lifted a good 2 metres into the air, and came down hard on my backside. I jumped up and started running, but she was in for seconds, and I was lifted again, probably another metre or so, before landing on the same spot, which was turning red raw very quickly. The cow left me then, and ran over to her calf.

Simone was screaming from the fence: 'You all right, Troy? You right?'

'Of course I'm not bloody right! Come and give me a hand,' I shouted back.

But she'd seen enough to know she wasn't setting foot in that paddock. So I hobbled back to her feeling sorry for myself, and we walked back together to the homestead.

When we told Dad what happened, he said, 'Crazy old cow for doing that. She knows she's looked after, that she's got a pretty good life.' He was even smiling about how good a life that old cow had till Mum caught his eye and he became serious again.

So he got a bit of plastic hose, and he took me back into the paddock again with him. I walked in his footsteps right behind him, thinking, really proud, that my Dad was going to teach that cow a lesson for hurting his son.

When the cow came flat out for Dad he gave her a smack on the nose with the hose-length. She turned around, got the calf in beside her and ran straight into the yard where we wanted her. She was happy enough munching on a sheet of hay, and I'm sure she was laughing at me as she and her calf looked on without a care. But I was really proud of my Dad. 'Yeah,' I thought. 'That's my Dad. No one messes with *him*.'

❖ ❖ ❖

Dad got me out of a few scrapes at Waite River, one way or another. During school holidays once, I had my cousin Wayne to stay. One morning Wayne and I, being as annoying as young boys can be around the house playing games, mistakenly walked across Mum's new seedlings in her vegetable garden.

Mum went mad at us then she sent us both down to give Dad a hand and annoy him in the cattle yards. She must have had a word or two with Dad, I reckon, though I never saw it happen. I guess it was one of those things parents can do, via telepathy or something.

Whatever it was, Dad must've known we needed to get some energy out, because he got Wayne and me to push up a cranky old cow from the main yard to the receiving yard.

'Stand your ground,' he said. 'Don't let her know you're frightened or she'll put it over you. She's not going to hurt you.'

Wayne and I looked at each other wondering why the other stockmen weren't standing their ground being men.

Every time we went to go on the rail Dad kept on at us. I reckon that's how I developed a knack for clowning around. I had to face that crazy cow and get around without her touching me – call her bluff and step aside.

I always respected Dad for making me stand my ground, because learning the right moves has saved my life on a few occasions.

Anyway, I must've got it into my head I knew all the tricks, because the next day I went down to give Dad a hand again. In no time I was all dusty, looking and feeling like a real stockman shifting cattle like I'd done it all my life.

I was walking along pushing some cattle up to a ramp to

load them onto the truck there, right behind an old bullock. I was using a length of plastic pipe to push him along, just like Dad had used on that milking cow.

I got him into the far end of the forcing pen leading up to the race and turned to chain the gate shut. But this old fella spun around and came straight at me. Luckily he didn't have big horns – he was what we call a knobby – but it was all bone in there that knocked me into the rails. He wouldn't stop, either, and I couldn't go anywhere because I was up against the corner of the yard. He hit me quite a few times before I could get a chance to crawl beneath the rails. I came out with a smashed-up nose, some skin off my cheeks and a black eye for good measure.

Dad saw what was happening from outside the yard. The fences were 2 metres high, and what I remember most clearly was Dad just putting his hands on the top of one rail and jumping the whole thing in one bound.

He must have done it without having to think, because when he saw what was happening he would have had to believe I was going to be hurt badly. Dad got to me just as I came out of the yard.

I kept saying, 'It's all right, Dad, I'm not crying, I'm not crying.'

I'd learnt the difference between a sulking animal and a wild one. With a wild one, you can tell what he's going to do because he shows it in his eyes, his face, his stance. But a sulking one won't show what's getting his blood up, but it's building up slow and mean all the same. He looks quiet enough, till, out of nowhere, he'll turn on you and hurt you.

But it was Dad's amazing reaction that impressed me then

and still does, when I think about it. Talk about strength when you're under pressure!

I saw it another time when I was with Dad trucking some wild cattle. One stood out a mile – it wanted to kill anything in its sight. A truck driver pulled up at the loading ramp and I distinctly remember Dad saying to him, 'You better put this bullock into the small pen on his own up there, because he'll horn, bruise and hurt the other animals. And don't get in the trailer with him, he's too mean.'

Well the bullock came flat out up the race and into the truck. He turned and saw the truck driver, who thought he knew better than to take Dad's advice, standing at the top of the loading ramp, trying to shut the gates on the trailer when the bullock turned around and horned him.

We all ran over to help get him out, but before anyone was close, Dad was up in there in a flash. He lifted the driver up over the loading ramp gates in one great heave.

I'll never forget it, because the truck driver would have weighed around 90 kilograms – he wasn't a small bloke – and Dad would have needed amazing strength to do it.

The driver spent the next couple of weeks in hospital and the doctors said he was lucky to be alive.

❖   ❖   ❖

Not all accidents out here are caused by wild bulls or speeding bikes. There was the time that love broke my – ear.

I'd set my heart on a particular governess. But governesses tended to come and go, for all sorts of reasons, and this young lady had moved on. She'd been off the station for a while when she let us know she was coming to visit.

When I heard she'd arrived, I ran up from the work shed.

As I ran I could see she was over in the garden with Mum, who was watering her flowers and vegetables. I had butterflies in my stomach, and I was running along, not looking where I was going. Smiling and waving to her, I ran full tilt, smack, bang into a 6-metre steel bore pipe that was sticking out the back of the four-wheel-drive, cutting my right ear in half at the top. Blood was everywhere.

As Mum and the governess bandaged me up, I felt like a total fool. Luckily for me, Mum knew a thing or two about first aid. I guess with me around she had no choice.

We all learnt a bit of first aid, but Mum usually took charge when someone hurt themselves although she reckons she wasn't a good nurse as she hated blood.

Mum wasn't always on the nursing side of station accidents. Once, at the same old yards where that sulky bullock turned on me, Mum was helping us do some branding of the new calves, heating the irons on the branding fire just inside the main yard.

Mum was leaning over to get the brand when a big mickey (a young weaner bull) came flying out from the main mob and hit her square on the backside. He sent her clean over the fire.

Dad's face went completely white, and he broke another land-speed record getting over to her.

As it turned out, it was lucky the mickey hit her as hard as he did. A bit softer and she'd have landed in the fire.

It shook the hell out of Mum. But these days, years later, we can all see the funny side of all those bumps and scrapes.

CHAPTER 7

THE MUSTER

Like most kids, I loved school holidays at Waite River. Because, during holidays in the dry season, I could go mustering and bull catching with Dad.

This is where I wanted to be. I remember the first time I went. Mum cooked up some cakes and treats for the boys, packed our bags, and we headed off to meet up with Dad.

Wherever Dad was he'd usually have the stock camp set up near an old creek bed close to some sleeping old ghost gums. The stockmen's swags were down close to the creek. I put out my swag alongside them but a little higher up on the greyish-brown clay soil.

That night felt like my first real experience of station life where it counts – out on the land working the stock and seeing that they survive whatever it is Nature throws up.

Dad woke me up at five o'clock the next morning with a cheery 'Wakey, wakey, hands off snakey. Tucker's up, Troy.

Breakfast, mate' (I didn't know what he was on about for a couple of years). Well, breakfast hadn't touched the sides before we were all out catching our horses.

A good deal of the hard work for this muster had been done. We had portable panels because we didn't have many stationary yards established back then. It'd take half a day, a full one sometimes, to pull all these panels together where you could hold a couple of thousand head of cattle.

The panels were heavy for a young kid, but I couldn't wait to carry them around like Dad and the men. Dad thought I should wait a year or two before trying to lift the portable panels, just as he thought I should wait before trying to start bore motors, but whenever I knew he wasn't watching I'd give it a go. Dad didn't approve because I could hurt my back, but it didn't worry me then (although later on in life it would!).

The yards were built and every thing was set. Now all we needed was the cattle to go in them.

My Dad was one of the first people in central Australia to use helicopters, and what with ten or twelve stockmen on horses and a bull catcher or two on the ground, mustering was a big job of coordination. The horse riders would go out and the helicopters would bring in the stock from further beyond for the riders to gather together.

Dad would probably be in a bull catcher chasing down the rogue scrubber bulls that were trying to slip the noose. Most often I'd ride with him, hanging on for dear life as the chase got hairy, which it often did. We were catching the tough buggers, and they'd give us a good run for our money.

This particular paddock was over 50,000 hectares, and that first day we had stock coming in from all points of the compass.

The plan was to get them to a waterhole halfway back to the portable panel yard, where we'd pull them up for dinner camp.

Well, what with the choppers being able to go out as far as they could, there were some pretty wild bulls being brought in from way out. Some were frothing at the mouth. They didn't want to be caught and were trying just about everything they could to avoid it.

The main part of the mob was moving quietly enough. Dad had first started off with coacher cattle. Coacher cattle are beasts that have been brought in a while before, and have become a bit more domesticated from being around horses and humans. So that was pretty much under control.

But the wilder fellas are always going to be trouble. You handle them with bull catchers, utility vehicles with old tyres strung across the front of them as padding. This way you can bump the odd bull like a big old dodgem car to get it back into the coacher mob or into a yard if it doesn't want to go.

With a steady man at the wheel, the bull catcher is priceless. Dad's a good man at the job.

This first time out for me was like my apprenticeship. But at the same time I'm sure Dad wanted to keep me out of too much trouble, so he kept me with him till we came in for lunch. There are always ringers still out with the mob, while the others eat and drink billy tea that never tasted so good, even to a bloke whose own brew got a ribbon on it at school get-together day. And then we'd switch places, all taking turns. The cattle are always watched over, but no one goes without a feed or a spell.

With everyone fed, and the cows mothered up with their calves, Dad had us all moving quick smart so that it wouldn't be much past late afternoon before we were ready to yard the cattle up.

Jackaroos and jilleroos (roos, for short) ride behind the tail of a mob. That's where you learn the trade, but you're in the dust all the time. Later on you get to work the wing and up front. Back there that day I could hardly see. Dust was all over my face, everywhere, dirt across my teeth, as I just poked along, pushing the stragglers to keep up.

I kept a special eye out for the calves, because the young ones feel the length of the day most of all, and they get a bit tired and start to lose their mothers. You have to be careful because if a calf wants to run away it will head back to where it had its last drink of milk, which might be kilometres back.

Dad pulled up the bull catcher alongside me and a few other stockmen who were on the tail. 'Keep those calves with their mothers, mate. It's the biggest job of the day.' That was my responsibility, to make sure no calves wandered off, got themselves lost and just as likely died out there on their own.

Dad would put any calf that was really tired and wasn't able to keep walking in the bull catcher with him, and he'd drive it the rest of the way to the yard. The days were hot enough and long enough, so sometimes he might end up with six or seven of the little blokes getting a chauffeured ride back to their mums.

My first day was a big one, and there was no way I was coming out of the saddle or making a beeline for home or my last good feed, even if I was daydreaming at times and trying not to fall asleep. I had a job to do, I'd been entrusted with it, and dusty and bone-weary as I might be, I was working side by side with my dad. I wouldn't have been anywhere else on earth.

I've ridden a lot of hours mustering after that, and I reckon I've got a few more ahead of me. But, you know, much as the job is similar every time, it's completely different day to day.

Because that's how quickly a situation can change – between one look at the lie of the land and the next.

I remember one time when we got to the yard and there were probably fifteen or twenty wild bulls that plain flat refused to go in. I would have been about eight or nine years old. I was in the old bull catcher with Dad. Mose and Colin were in the back. Colin was about fourteen at the time.

So, we were all in the bull catcher chasing down one of these mean buggers, and Dad was wheeling around after him, this way and that. I looked back at Mose and Colin hanging on to the rails for dear life. They were almost flying – they looked like cartoon characters, their feet up in mid-air out the side as Dad swung around another corner. It was just as well, probably, because in the back of the bull catcher the tucker box, the spare tyre and the jack were bouncing around, hard and heavy enough to collect them well and truly.

Dad had done a fair few big dusty doughnuts wheeling around, and the bull catcher's engine was screaming like mad as we chased down one big bull. He was a huge Shorthorn Brahman cross, close to 1000 kilograms in weight. He had big horns sticking way out, and right between them a mean look in his eyes that said there was no way he was going into the yard. I remember that look, because he turned around to face us. Then he charged the bull catcher. He probably had a bone to pick with all of us, but I remember him fixing that blood-shot look fair on me.

We were out in the middle of nowhere, flat, nothing to

put between us and a filthy-mad mountain of meat except one little stripling of a whitewood tree. Dad pulled up alongside it and told Mose and Colin to jump off. They would be safer there because everything was getting thrown around too much in the back.

Mose went to grab the branch to climb on it. It was fairly thin, and it bent half over as soon as he grabbed hold of it. Suddenly, Colin grabbed the branch up further, and he stepped on Mose's head to push off him and get up the tree as fast as he could. Poor old Mose slid down the tree while Colin scampered up it.

Meanwhile, Dad had taken off after the bull. The thing is, this mean old bull was either meaner than we thought, or it had a funny bone buried somewhere in all that muscle. Because it lined up the tree with the two blokes scrambling up it. By the time Mose and Colin had both got as far to the top of this young tree as they could they had bent it right down like a boomerang, so that it was hanging over a metre or two from the ground.

But the old bull mustn't have been able to move for confusion. He didn't know what to look at: the bull catcher or Colin and Mose. He could have rushed up and knocked them both into next week, but Dad wheeled to the right, pushing him towards the yard, the tyres on the front taking the full weight of the obstinate brute. He refused to go in the yard, but every time we got a bit closer.

In the end, Dad just knocked him down and told me to jump out of the car and grab his tail over his flank as he pinned him down. Simple as that. A thousand kilograms plus of bull and me, 40 kilograms max those days, helping hold him down. But I'd seen it done before, so I went down there and grabbed hold of the tail between his back legs. It doesn't leave a knocked-down bull too many places to go, so long as you can hold onto that tail and lean back. I got that bit right, because Dad had time to back the bull catcher up and tie his legs up with a leather strap. After tipping the points off his horns, the main mob would be brought over and the bull let up to join his mates.

Meanwhile, Mose and Colin climbed down from that tree – stepped down probably, it was bent over so far – and came up to join us.

Sometimes bulls are left tied up just until the truck comes to get them if the coachers are too far away. The stockmen then hook a rope on to the bull's horns and winch it up the ramp onto the back of the truck. Then you can get it off to that yard it didn't want to walk into in the first place.

The thing is, like any job, you get to do the same thing over and over, but when you're dealing with living creatures, there's always the chance things will be a little – or maybe a whole lot – different to what they were last time. It keeps you on your toes, knowing everything you've ever done before is only good for getting you through what's about to come as long as you keep your wits about you. Slack off, go into automatic, and you might find yourself with a face full of dust. Or worse, a bellyful of horn.

I remember another time, when I was out contract mustering with Dad. Again, Dad told me to get off the bull catcher, because everything was being thrown around.

While Dad went off to chase down the bull, I was out there surrounded by nothing but the blue horizon and red dirt, with two small gidgee trees to break the view on the outskirts of the muster. There were cattle coming in from all directions and the sound of choppers filled the sky so that I didn't really know where to look. With my back to the yards a couple of kilometres away, I watched as the cattle strung out in a trot only a stone's throw away, straight past me.

Then I heard him, a wild looking scrubber with big horns and a brown and white woolly forehead. It had obviously got to the yards and decided, 'I'm out of here.' And now I seemed to be standing in his way to freedom. I froze. I was on the outskirts of the open granite plain a few metres from the gidgee trees, and he was a few metres on the other side, wanting to be where I was. Well I'd have swapped him places in a heart's beat, but as that wasn't possible we were checkmate.

I had to think quickly: if I ran out on to the plain without any tree to get behind he was sure to get me in his path, but if I ran for the tree I may beat him. So I took my chance and ran for it towards him. He must have been as frightened as I was, because he started coming head down and flat out at me. I panicked and turned around trying to set a new ground-speed record running while looking over my shoulder all the time, but he was closing in on me every step of the way.

Dad had always said (jokingly) that if a bull charges at you, reach down its throat and grab his tail, pull him inside out, and he'll run the other way. But as good as Dad's advice sounded, I could now feel the breath of his nostrils on my backside. I ducked left 90 degrees and fooled him, but now I was faced with his rear end and him turning himself back towards me. I'd seen full-grown men do it so I grabbed for his tail and hung on like there was no tomorrow. I figured I was safer this end than the pointy end.

He flung me everywhere. I might as well have been with

Dad still being tossed around in the tray of the bull catcher for the rattling my brains were getting. But there was no way I was going to let go of that tail, because if I did he was going to hurt me, nothing more was certain. So I hung on, keeping his body between me and those wicked horns and keeping to his side, so as not to get kicked by his back legs, all the time trying to run him around in these little semi-circles to get us closer and closer to the tree.

As luck had it we worked our way back so we were within a couple of metres of it, me with a mouthful of dust, my hands aching like crazy and my heart beating clean out of my chest. I let go and made a dart for it. I reckon he was closer to me than my shadow, because I'd just stepped around the tree when he went past and kept going.

I watched him all the way till he disappeared out of sight. I was still hugging the gidgee tree like it was my new best friend. The sound of the choppers got closer.

Half an hour later Dad came by in the bull catcher and told me to get in quickly. Without a minute to spare I was telling him about my close shave. I was talking so quickly I must have lost Dad there somewhere, and I'm sure he had other things on his mind, because he said, 'Jump in, mate. We'll finish yarding up and then you can tell me your story.'

❖ ❖ ❖

Still the station 'apprentice' at ten years old, on one occasion I was bringing up a mob of twenty or thirty back-up horses called 'the plant'. Riders usually need two or three horses a day to do a big muster, because the horses get tired from travelling long distances. The riders switch horses at lunchtime and again at dusk if you're going far into the night.

I was about a kilometre behind the main herd, where horses and a chopper were bringing cattle in from all sides. Daydreaming as I rode along, I passed a clump of witchetty bush. Before I knew it a Hereford cross bull was coming at me.

He gored the horse in the stomach, and it collapsed under me. Even though I managed to roll away, I wasn't much better off than the horse. I was face to face with the bull, which was eyeing me with the kind of look that freezes you in your tracks. But instead of putting in the effort to clean me up, he just walked off.

I hated that bull. Those wild bulls know exactly what they're up to when they charge you. With tears in my eyes, I got my saddle off the horse as quickly as I could. One of the stockmen came along in the bull catcher. He had to shoot my mount with a rifle from a rack in his vehicle to put it out of its misery.

I felt terrible. I raised the saddle over my shoulder, but it was almost as big as me, so the stockman gave me a lift to catch up with the rest of the horses.

I saddled up another horse and got on with the job. What else could I do? But I felt so sad for the horse we had to put down. That was the last time I would ever daydream, I promised myself. From now on I'd keep my wits about me.

It was one occasion – and there have been a few since – when a gun's power to take life quickly and cleanly is the only thing that has stood between a suffering creature and an agonising death, whether it's been an injured horse suffering pain or a native animal on the edge of the highway, fallen victim to a careless driver. The fact is, guns used safely are a necessity of life in the bush.

ABOVE: My great uncles Fred (far left)and Ted Colson (far right) on the edge of the Simpson Desert displaying a goanna caught while on a 'dogging' trip aimed at controlling the dingo population.

LEFT: After it had been said it couldn't be done, in 1936 my great uncle Ted Colson crossed the Simpson Desert. My family history is dotted with men and women I can look back to for inspiration.

BELOW: Building yards was hard yakka in Fred Colson's day. Here he and his fellow station workers cut the timber on site using a portable saw.

LEFT: Mum and Dad's wedding in 1964. Their strong and committed relationship has carried them through the many hardships they've had to face on the land and their love is still just as strong today. I'm lucky to have had their love and support through all my ups and downs.

BELOW: Old Mose worked at Waite River while I was growing up and had an influence on me, teaching me a few tricks about the land.

LEFT: At the age of 2 on one of my first sets of wheels – an early sign of my continuing passion for bikes.

BELOW: Dad looks on with an amused grin after giving me my first ride on station horse 'Bibby' at Waite River. I was later to graduate from fluffy slippers to boots and spurs.

LEFT: My passion for bikes was only equalled by my passion for horses. Here I am at about 4 riding Dad's horse 'Big Smoke' at Waite River, my legs trying hard to reach to the stirrups.

LEFT: By age 5, on our family pony 'Licorice', I could join Dad on his rides around the property to help muster cattle, and generally work the land.

RIGHT: Me on 'Powder Puff' (left), my first horse after 'Licorice', with Simone on her horse 'Pesky' at Waite River.

ABOVE: Snakes are part of everyday life in the Outback. I found this skeleton of a king brown snake in the shed on our property when I was 10.

LEFT: (L-R) Pansy McLeod, Hilda Bird and Mavis Bird who used to help mum in the station homestead at Waite River and were good friends while we were growing up.

My middle sister Tanya (7), big sis Simone (12) and me (10) at Waite River wearing some of mum's homemade clothes. It was a great life being a station kid.

LEFT: Me at around 14, during my boarding school days. Nice haircut, Troy!

BELOW: Mum teaching my youngest sister Heidi (at age 5) how to use School of the Air. Mum's poodle, Monnie lends her support.

Photo courtesy of Northern Territory Department of Education

Long-haired lout at 17! With a mate on a rare Sunday break at Great Keppel after looking at Brahman cattle on nearby Queensland properties.

Admiring the great Monaro that I bought when I was 18

Working commercial stock at Amburla, looking for a suntan! (I was about 20 here).

With Uncle Scottie (centre) and Dad (right) at my 21st.
The theme was 'Tarts and Tramps' – one wild party

Me in 1989, age 22, on the back of the first Brahman stud bull, 'Lancefield Indu Jester', that we bought from Queensland. It was the beginning of our first introduced bloodlines at Amburla.

Road trains are an essential part of Outback life in transporting large numbers of stock to market over vast distances. This one is a mere 150 metres long!

My three wonderful sisters, Simone (top) who stars in 'Outback Adventures', Tanya the super mum (middle) and Heidi (bottom) who does a wonderful job as my personal assistant, keeping me up-to-date and on track.

ABOVE: My good friend Rex (left) and me
showing off our Champion Bull and Cow at
the Alice Springs Show. They went on to also
win Champion Interbreed.

RIGHT: Country shows are an important part
of life in the Outback – a great social meeting
place and for showing your stock to help you
get sales.

The family's little gem of a plane, M.L.P., a Cessna 182Q, always ready to fly, as seen here at Amburla airstrip. From mustering stock and spotting, to aerial work and travelling, we enjoyed more than 1500 hours flying together.

M.L.P. looking a little sad after our crash due to engine failure, but still a gem – after all, I'm still here to tell you my story.

LEFT: Working the land, repairing old stock yards. This is one of the photographs that led to filming the series pilot 'Our Country' that went on to become 'Outback Adventures'.

BELOW: Motorbikes play an important role on properties, from mustering stock to checking fences and bores. They are cheap to maintain and cheap on fuel – a fast mechanical horse.

LEFT: On location filming 'Our Country', the pilot program I took to Cannes, with some friends that I grew up with at Waite River joining in on the fun while shooting scenes at Amburla.

MIDDLE: My good friend Bill who helped produce and direct 'Outback Adventures' and is now co-producer on the movie *Outback Legend*.

Photo by Bill Leimbach
for Becker Entertainment

BELOW: Me directing a shot on 'Outback Adventures' – finally fulfilling a dream.

Photo by Bill Leimbach
for Becker Entertainment

In the Buccaneer Archipelago on the north coast of Western Australia. We were filming
a story for 'Outback Adventures' about a unique Aussie family who make a living off
commercial barramundi fishing. Also one of our favourite sporting fish, the barra share these
waters with some of the biggest crocodiles in the land.

Photo by Bill Leimbach for Becker Entertainment

So I was back on a horse with the same job still needing doing. On we went, right into the evening.

The roadtrains that were coming in to truck out the cattle were due in at two in the morning, so Dad set up a little generator to power the floodlights in the yards.

Drafting at night is quite dangerous: you're surrounded by wild cattle, which seem to double in number as every shadow and dark patch takes on the appearance of a wild bull. If ever you had to grow eyes in the back of your head, it's when you're working at night.

And then what a job – trucking cattle from two o'clock till daylight. Dad would make breakfast, and then keep going, mustering through the next day. The blokes who worked for Dad were always paid well and were fed and looked after. But they worked long hours, so there was always a bit of a joke around the country: 'That Garry Dann, you earn your tucker with him', and 'You've got to get up early in the morning to beat Garry Dann.' They were always respectful, though, because people know how much difference a good boss makes on the job, and there weren't too many who didn't sign up again when Dad was hiring.

The worst part for me back then wasn't the dust and flies, or the accidents, soreness or everything else that went with being in the saddle for long hours. The worst thing was the day when I was put on the roadtrain to go back home because school was about to start again.

I'd say goodbye to Dad and the stockmen, tired, dirty and dusty, but all the time I was hoping Dad would say, 'Nah, blow that, you stay out here. We need the extra man.' I could see he was proud of the work I'd put in, but he knew better than me that my education was more important, and that the work is everywhere, and the extra man never goes to waste, wherever he is.

So Dad would say to me, knowing full well Mum was okay, 'You have to go back home and make sure Mum and everyone's all right,' as if he was relying on me to see everyone through at home. That made me feel pretty good, no matter how bad I was feeling about going back in.

Then he'd give me the clincher: 'Troy, you've got to keep up those times tables. I'll be testing you when I get home.' There was no answer to that, because, of course, I'd let them fall away a little out on the job, and those twelve times tables used to trip me up badly. Dad would know how hard I'd been putting in at the school work by testing my twelve times tables.

So, home I'd go, and home was where it was last time, and it sure looked good. There'd be lots of adventures to have around the place, which would pass the time along with school work. Dad would be back, too, in no time, and I could look forward to the next muster.

CHAPTER 8

....

BOARDING SCHOOL

I think back to those years of my childhood at Waite River, and it seems like one long unbroken time, full of incident but grounded by being in one place with the same people right through. There's not a day of those memories I'd trade for gold.

But time has a habit of flashing by, and things do change, even if it's little by little. Heidi, my youngest sister, was born, and kept us all on our toes, especially Mum. Then Simone went off to boarding school, leaving just Tanya and me attending School of the Air. Mum and Dad continued to work Waite River, but I know Dad still had his dream, somewhere in his heart, of one day buying Amburla Station.

And then I was twelve years old and following in Simone's footsteps, leaving Waite River Station for an adventure shared by so many other Outback kids – boarding school in the big smoke.

And did it change my life!

Mum and Dad always wanted the best for us kids, so my bags were packed and I was shipped south 1500 kilometres to Scotch College in Adelaide.

It was not only a sad time for us kids. I'll never forget the look on Mum's face as Simone and I boarded the plane. She was trying to smile through her tears and was telling us we'd be okay. Mum knew that what they were doing was best for us, but it didn't take away the pain of letting us go. Although she still had my two younger sisters – Tanya, who was now nine, and Heidi, who was three – the emptiness in that old house now both Simone and I were gone would have been hard for her to come to terms with.

❖   ❖   ❖

Adelaide, the capital of South Australia, is known as the City of Churches. It's also famous for the arts festival held there every two years, which attracts some of the best artists and writers in the world. Recently, the city has become the site for WOMADELAIDE, a festival attended by musicians from all over the planet.

Adelaide features large in Australian history, because many of the expeditions that set out into the Red Centre started from there, or aimed to end up there, or both. So there are a lot of monuments around the city commemorating successful – and sometimes tragically unsuccessful – explorations.

It's a pretty place, set between the Mount Lofty Ranges and the waters of Gulf St Vincent. The next land you hit south of the Gulf is Antarctica, so while Adelaide isn't at the very bottom of the Australian continent, it's the last city in a line south of Alice Springs that you can get to without getting your feet wet.

People who fancy cities reckon Adelaide's got a lot going

for it, with the Torrens River running through the middle, the old buildings and the culture, which is kept chugging along by the festivals. Each to their own, I suppose, because most of my memories of the place are of my school years there, and they were not the best time of my life.

Scotch College has a lot of tradition behind it, stretching back to its foundation just after the First World War, partly in memory of all the Australians of Scottish ancestry who fought and died in that conflict. The school has a reputation for academic excellence as well as a long history of educating Outback kids in the boarding schools for both boys and girls.

It sprawls across two properties sitting side by side and totalling 20 hectares in the Torrens Park area of Mitcham, about 8 kilometres south of the city, just in the foothills of the Mount Lofty Ranges. My sister Simone had been there two years by the time I started and, thanks to her, our name was well-regarded in the school.

Simone had grown into quite an attractive young woman, with long brunette hair, big, warm, green eyes and an outgoing personality. She'd settled in well by her third year at the school. I could tell all this because all the boys seemed to be after her.

Simone boarded in the girls' dormitories about 2 kilometres from where I was staying. It was great she was there at school with me: it meant I had a friend to talk to, because I grew awfully homesick during the first few months at school.

Andy Hayes was another friend starting at Scotch College in the same year. He was a shy, good-looking kid of medium build with fair hair. Andy and I had completed primary school through the School of the Air together, so we knew each other pretty well without having seen one another all that often.

Andy lived about 270 kilometres south-west of Waite River

on a property called Undoolya. Andy's family were among the first European settlers to pioneer Central Australia.

Undoolya is nestled in under the beautiful eastern Mac-Donnell Ranges. Painters, photographers and writers often come to record the landscape and the life forms resident there, and have a lifetime ahead of them without ever finishing the job. Deceptively flat and uninviting, the red soil escarpments, gaps and gorges of this part of the Centre are home to many species of hardy plants and perhaps even hardier animals, as well as some amazing birds, including my favourite, the wedge-tailed eagle, Australia's largest bird of prey with a wing-span of up to 2.5 metres. Besides the wedgetail, there are galahs, cockatiels, pigeons, doves, sulphur-crested cockatoos, red-tailed black cockatoos and budgerigars, thrushes and grass wrens. Because the region is well served for water, with creeks and waterholes, you can also find water-seeking bird life like the Pacific heron, fairy martin and black-fronted plover. The list goes on before you even start to look underfoot at the insects, reptiles and marsupials that also live there.

Like many of the kids who came from the land, Andy and I shared a few twelve-year-old tears during our first days at boarding school.

On our first day in Adelaide, Andy and I caught a taxi together from the airport. We arrived at the college to be greeted by our boarding house master. Mr Brown had a dark beard covering most of his face and piercing eyes that seemed to stare straight through you when he was angry.

'Put your bags in there. That's your bed, and that's yours. Keep your area tidy at all times. The bathroom is down the hall. Homework is in the study from 7 p.m. to 8 p.m. Clean your teeth and lights out by 8.30.'

We just nodded. 'Yes, Mr Brown.' I wondered whether it was like this in an army camp. I put my bag on the bed and started unpacking, looking across at Andy doing the same, when three other boys who shared the same room came over.

They said they'd been there a year already and that they were in charge, so we had to abide by their rules. I looked across at Andy again and we ignored the comment. But by that stage they had moved on to tell some other newcomer the same thing.

Later that night I lay in bed listening to the strange sound of vehicles travelling along a nearby road, trying to ignore a pillow fight that was going on next to my bed. I was staring at the ceiling when the door swung wide open, revealing Mr Brown.

'Get to sleep. If I catch anyone out of bed they'll be on dishes duty for a week,' he barked.

The door closed and we were in darkness again. All was quiet for at least a couple of minutes. Then *bang*, something stung my ear. Someone across the room had used a rubberband slingshot to fire a paper bullet, and they'd shot a bullseye. Just as I yelled at the culprit in walked Brown. So I was washing dishes for a week.

During breakfast next morning I got my share of bagging from the gang of toughies, who were saying things like 'Don't forget to do the dishes, Troy.'

Andy and I headed off on our kilometre walk to school. On the way I spotted the boy who had stung me with the paper slug.

I fronted him: 'You know you could have deafened me, and you got me into trouble last night.'

'I don't care,' he said.

'What do you mean you don't care?' I asked him.

'I don't care.'

I couldn't believe he'd say this to me! My blood pumping, I walked over and punched him in the mouth. He fell to the ground and just lay there, not moving. Within seconds, everyone was around him in a circle looking down at him.

'You've killed him!' said one kid.

Shocked, I walked on to school, not looking back once, wondering how long I was going to spend in jail.

I was sitting outside the chapel on a bench, my head in my hands, when Andy came running up. 'It's all right, mate. You just knocked him out. He's awake now.'

That was a relief, I can tell you. I was the talk of the school that day, when all I wanted was to be back home on my motor bike doing a bore run away from everyone. Instead, I was at boarding school and I'd got off on the wrong foot on day one. From then on I seemed to always be in trouble.

I think I was just a square peg in a round hole. I could never get used to the blazer and tie with shiny black shoes we had to wear each day. Everything felt too tight and too straight, and it seemed as if what really mattered was how you looked, not what qualities you had in you.

I also didn't like coming second because I'd always thought that second was the first loser. But I hadn't played much team sports like football and cricket, so learning the ropes in year eight was tough, and getting into the B team instead of the A team was a shame job to me!

I decided to try my hand at rowing, and found out it was just my cup of tea. Before long I held the record for my year on the rowing machine in the gymnasium, recording the most strokes per minute.

But while I excelled in rowing, I was still getting into trouble, no matter how hard I tried to avoid it. Once, we were dissecting frogs in a biology class. The teacher told the class that frogs live under the ground for weeks on end in the wild till the rain comes and then they crawl to the surface.

One girl asked, 'How long can they live without rain? A couple of years?'

'Not that long,' said the teacher.

Hearing this, I put my hand up and said, 'Sorry, but they can. I've seen it in bad droughts.'

So much for local knowledge getting me anywhere. 'Go and sit in the corner, you cheeky boy,' was the teacher's reply.

This confused me. Why was I getting punished? I didn't think I'd done or said anything wrong, or that I was being cheeky by correcting the teacher. I'd been brought up well, and had been taught good manners. I was only debating the subject, just like I'd always done growing up around adults for most of my life.

I started to find it harder and harder to fit in to the school's way of doing things. I decided I needed to discuss the situation with Simone, so after tea we met up behind the woodwork shed, where she and her friends often sneaked away for a cigarette before returning to their boarding house.

'Cool,' I thought. With a pack of cigarettes in my hip pocket, I'd always thought I was Marlboro man himself. Back on the station, once, I was out riding PowderPuff and we had to get to the top of a hill to look around for stray cattle. So I'd cantered to the top humming the Marlboro tune to myself the whole way up: 'dant da da dant, da da da dada dant, dant da da dant, da da da dada dant.' Reaching the top I'd lit up and surveyed the land below. I'd thought I was so cool!

So there I was behind the woodwork shed, sucking on a cigarette, telling Simone how much I didn't like school. There must have been a hoodoo on me because, out of nowhere, Mr Brown appeared and sprung us.

I was suspended for a week. Mum and Dad were furious. 'We spend hard-earned money to give you the best education we can, and this is how you repay us?'

I felt terrible. I knew I'd disappointed my parents, so after spending a week away with my auntie and uncle, I returned, determined to keep my head down and get good grades for Mum.

I tried to study harder, which must have impressed someone because when I asked for permission to leave school grounds on afternoons and weekends to find pocket money work doing odd jobs around the neighbourhood, I was given it straight away.

After a few false starts, and once I worked out I needed to negotiate terms before doing the job, the pocket money started to roll in. A couple of times the extra effort I put into jobs even earned a tip, and I felt proud of how well my little business was doing.

Things also started to go a lot better at school, especially now I knew when to keep quiet. The world wouldn't stop turning if some frog didn't dig its way back up to water after a big drought out in the bush or in some city teacher's cock-eyed textbook.

I'd finally made it into the A team in Aussie Rules football, even though I spent most of the time on the bench, and I'd been chosen to row in the prestigious Head of the River with one of the school's top teams!

But first I had to try out for athletics. I ranked highly in the javelin and discus, my throwing action probably sharpened by those years of hunting with my Aboriginal mates. But I fared less well in the long jump, which favoured the taller blokes. And it was when I tried out for the long jump that everything turned bad for me again.

Angus was a six-feet-tall Scottish dude in the same year I was in, who was good at track and field events. And here he was on the side of the sand pit laughing and pointing at me as I ran up to jump. I ignored him, picked myself up and dusted off, then went back to line up again. He kept it up – and I kept ignoring him.

Then, just as I got close to the jump line again, he started bagging my friends. Instead of leaping into the sand pit, I jumped to the side and knocked him clean over! I was sent straight back to the boarding house.

My mate Urlam and I headed home via the locker room, but as we approached the door, there was Angus waiting for me.

I told him I wasn't looking for trouble, not from him or anyone else. I was in enough trouble for today already. I just wanted to pick up my homework and go and do it.

But Angus wasn't having any of that. If I wanted my homework I'd have to go through him to get it. I turned to Urlam, and Angus kicked me fair in the knee. It didn't hurt much, but it was enough to throw the switch.

I punched him straight in the stomach, and as he doubled over, I caught him a couple of quick punches to that big mouth of his. He went down like the proverbial sack of spuds.

It was unlucky for him, because he was wearing braces on his teeth, and those punches of mine really cut up the inside of his lips. There was blood everywhere, and even though

Urlam was all excited about how we'd showed him, what I saw looking down at this big guy laid flat out bleeding was enough to make me sick.

I was never into fighting for its own sake. Sure, like most kids anywhere, I'd mucked around with my mates, white and black, having big battles and one-on-one matches like kids do. But there were always unwritten rules – honour and respect stuff that kids think are gentlemen's agreements – and all that stunting around was different to what had just happened with Angus.

I can say honestly that I've never gone looking for a fight for its own sake since that day. There's no mileage in beating someone up just for the sake of it. However big you might feel about getting the jump on a person who was never looking for a fight, the real loser is you if the only way you can feel big is by making other people feel small.

Urlam and I went back to the boarding house and went to the supper room for afternoon tea. I looked out the window and saw a teacher running across from the locker rooms. He came racing into the supper room and started screaming at me like mad.

He grabbed me and dragged me out into the hallway. Soon a crowd of boarders had gathered as the two of us tussled in the corridor. Finally I broke free of him and we both stood there, facing each other off.

He made me go to my room, clean up and get my blazer and tie on and wait for him. There was some skin off my knuckles, a little bit of damage, so I washed that up as best I could, dressed in the uniform and sat there, waiting.

Finally he came back and told me I was going to have to apologise to Angus's family for the damage I'd done to him.

The teacher had the grace to ask me what had actually happened, so I told him.

He drove me to the other side of Adelaide to apologise to Angus's mother and father, and it was one of the longest journeys I can ever remember, and I've travelled more than a million miles since.

I felt really horrible about what I'd done to their son but, you know, nothing's ever as simple as black and white.

Still, whatever I might've thought about the rights and wrongs of fighting, the first result was I was grounded, and not allowed to take part in the Head of the River rowing competition for the school. Worse than that for a growing boy, I was also banned from going on school excursions, most importantly, to me, the weekly dancing lessons we took over at Seymour Girls College. I was pretty keen on a girl there, and it was tough punishment, I can tell you!

Sure, maybe I'd learnt my lesson, but for me that lesson was that sometimes the law is an ass, as some other bloke once put it. Like me, no doubt he got a hiding for his trouble!

CHAPTER 9

....

ONE BOTTLE OF
BRANDIVINO

I don't know what it was about boarding school. It felt as if it was set up to get you into trouble by making everything a cardinal sin inside the school gates that a young bloke – or a girl of the same age – might be doing out in the real world.

But here I was banned from just about anything except school work, homework, and thinking hard about how bad I'd been.

Luckily, my mate Dave and I got on particularly well with one of the tutors at the boarding house, and the tutor decided he'd give me a little room to move.

Dave was sweet on a girl over in the girls' dormitory, so he arranged with the tutor to leave the door in our dorm unlocked so we could go over to the girls. Dave could see her, say hello – it was pretty innocent stuff – and then we'd get back to our dorm without any problems.

Dave always had a romantic streak, so as we were going out he reckoned a bottle of wine might be in order. I knew that one teacher had a cellar full of the stuff. He was always heading out to the surrounding wine districts and bringing back carloads of wine on his free weekends. We snuck down to his cellar and borrowed a couple of bottles. I'd heard of a drink called Brandivino, so that was what we took. Lucky I wasn't a few years older, or the words Penfold's Grange might have been more familiar to me, and the teacher would have really lost out on Dave's romantic night.

Once the girls knew there were boys in their dorm, it turned into a bit of a party. Dave and his sweetheart got all familiar with each other on a beanbag, while the other girls in the room decided that Troy, with his two bottles of cheap wine, was the star of the evening. They passed around one bottle between them, while I was seriously slugging on the other one.

All of a sudden, there were lights in the corridor. The girls started running for cover. Dave was up out of the beanbag like a shot. I was over to the window like a slug – legless, full of a bottle of Brandivino. We both jumped out. Dave landed on his feet, and I hit the dirt head first. Now I had a touch of concussion and, mixed with the Brandivino, I wasn't thinking too straight, so I suggested we make a run for home past the gymnasium. Dave said that was too close to the girls' teacher's window, and that the long way home was the only safe route. Even in the state I was in I could see where he was coming from. But the big stretch of hedge alongside the public road beside the school would be perfect cover until the final dash for the boys' dormitory.

Napoleon couldn't have planned it with more military

precision – especially if he'd had a bottle of Brandivino in him at the time. Of course, Napoleon had his share of bad luck. Dave's and mine was that, at one in the morning, as we worked our way home through the dark, the only car on that road was a police car.

'Run for it!' I said. But we only got a hundred metres before they pulled us up and grilled us, including asking for our names.

All of a sudden I could see I was heading for expulsion and a plane ticket back to the Outback. Not the best of home-comings, I could see that.

The two constables delivered us back to the dorm, and we were sent off to our beds with the promise we'd be dealt with in the morning.

Well, the teacher passed that buck all the way to the top, because in no short order I was standing in the Principal's office, with Simone there for moral support and even throwing in a few pleas for mercy. But it was no use. I was expelled.

As luck would have it – good or bad, I still haven't made my mind up – Mum and Dad were in Adelaide on business. They could take charge of me from the school gates, so I wouldn't have to make the long trip home alone.

But as I sat on my bed, all packed up, feeling pretty low about everything and thinking I'd only been at the school for just over a year and a half, I heard two pairs of heavy feet coming down the dormitory corridor. I knew one pair was my dad's, and suddenly the thought of making that trip alone seemed the safer option.

Especially when I heard my dad's familiar growl outside the dormitory door: 'Where is the little shit?'

That was me. And I felt it, too, having let my parents down.

'You've done it this time, haven't you?' Dad said, shaking

his head at me. 'Your mum's really upset. Go on, put your bags in the car.'

The thought of having upset Mum was the worst thing of all. But I was fourteen years old and feeling hard done by, even if the last disaster had pretty much been of my own making, so there was no way I was going to cry.

My old man shook the teacher's hand and we drove off in the car to see Mum at the hotel. Dad never said a word the whole way, like he was what he was – very disappointed in me. But he couldn't have been more disappointed than I was about making Mum cry over her badly behaved son.

It was just my bad luck that the day Dad was in town on business some really evil bugger had got up to no good the day before. It was all over the newspapers, and Dad threw one in my lap after stopping at a shop.

'You're going to turn out just like that, the way you're going,' he said, nodding at the cover story. There was a picture of an 83-year-old woman bandaged around the head and face where she'd been bashed by some bloke who broke into her house. I couldn't believe my Dad really thought I had it in me to be as low as to do that to a defenceless old lady.

We arrived at the hotel room. Mum was there and she'd been crying, and she started up a little again once she saw me. She shook her head and left the room.

Dad had his swag with him, and he took out his big leather belt and gave me a good old flogging. It was probably the biggest hiding he ever gave me in his life. I knew I probably deserved it for stealing the $2 wine, as I had so much respect for my father, but it had the result of driving me even further into myself. That does have its good side, and I've always been able to rely on my own inner strength, but the down side is it can make me seem a little too self-reliant, which at that age was just the sort of thing that got up the noses of other kids.

I was already three-quarters of the way through year nine, so it was going to be pretty hard to get me into another school to round out that year. Dad decided to take me home and give me a job for the last three months of the year at $50 a week to have responsibility for maintaining the property's bores. That seemed like a pretty good idea to me. It was all I wanted to be doing, in fact.

But I was still smarting from feeling hard done by, and the sting of Dad's belt didn't fade too quickly either. So not long after I got home I packed my swag, saddled my horse and was all ready to head north and leave the station as Sidney Kidman had done many moons ago, when he was a year younger than I was.

At the age of thirteen he'd run away from home with only five shillings in his pocket and a lump in his throat. Kidman ended up creating a mighty cattle empire of more than a hundred stations, fighting droughts, bushfires, floods and plagues of vermin to do so. His enterprise and courage saw him return home with a huge fortune and knowledge that made him the legend he is today, the 'cattle king', the biggest land owner in Australia's history.

I'd ridden about 10 kilometres out when I sat down under a tree to boil the billy for a cup of tea. The sun was just setting and radiant colours were splashed across the landscape. Cockatoos and zebra finches were carrying on above me. The racket they made sounded pretty much like the inside of my head – clashing thought, anger and wounded pride. None of it settled down long enough for me to have any idea where I really stood in life, or in my family, which was pretty much the same thing, and what I really wanted to be doing with myself.

Then I heard a pair of Major Mitchell cockatoos overhead. These cockatoos mate for life, and this pair had a couple of chicks up there in a nest. Seeing them got me thinking about families and the sacrifices Mum and Dad had made for me, and how much they cared for my sisters and me, and I knew that running away wasn't really going to solve anything. It sure wouldn't mend any broken bridges.

So I rode home, got in after dark, and just said I'd been out. I never told anyone I'd actually been going on the Kidman long ride.

But I still wasn't very comfortable with Dad. In fact, we were pretty much strangers to each other for the next twelve months, with barely a word passing between us. I just went into myself, did the jobs I had to do around the station, all the while learning new things. It could've gone on forever, and I would have been half good at a lot of things, but I was not really getting anywhere to the best of my ability.

So Dad said I had to at least get through year ten at another school, which would be enough to qualify me for a trade apprenticeship. With that I'd have the minimum to give me some real choices about living and working where I wanted to be: I'd be on the land, not just drifting across it.

So in the new year I started at St Philip's College in Alice Springs. I put my head down and went for it, and by the end of year ten 'Troy Dann' was the name on the award for Diligence in Studies. I also came second in the whole school in the apprenticeship exam.

On prize night, I was all done up in my blazer and tie with Mum and Dad looking proud as Punch. It was a bit of a turn-around from the last time Dad had seen me in a blazer and tie.

From the moment my name was called out for that diligence prize, all the bad blood between Dad and me started to flow away and we eventually became best mates again. It's a partnership that's just got stronger and stronger over the years, and I thank my lucky stars that I put in the effort I did at St Philip's, or perhaps Dad and I would never have reconciled, and that sort of unhappiness would have stained both our lives forever.

Without too much let up after I'd finished year ten, Dad told me it was time to start thinking about which trade qualification I wanted to go for.

I was so happy we were getting on well again, and I said I wanted to follow in his footsteps and become a butcher. But Dad reckoned mechanical engineering would set me in better stead, both around a station and off it if I was ever looking for work in town. Dad could teach me anything I wanted to know about butchery, anyway.

I'd always been interested in cars and engines and all the oily, greasy stuff, right back to the days when I scrounged scrap metal and fixed the local Aborigines' cars, so it didn't take too much imagination on my part to see what Dad was getting at.

Of course, I can't discount that Dad knew all along what made his son tick. Not all of it, naturally, but I reckon he knew I loved the Outback and wanted to work here. And he knew that, in my heart, more than anything I wanted him to be proud of me. And I was going to make sure he was.

CHAPTER 10

A DREAM GERMINATES

Everyone has dreams. Dad had inherited his dream from his dad, Alfie Dann – to buy Amburla Station. Well, while Simone and I were at boarding school, Dad's dream had finally come true.

When I finished year ten I returned to our new property. Amburla was 300 kilometres south-west of Waite River and over twice its size, with big beautiful open plains that ran right up to the foot of the MacDonnell Ranges.

It was so great to be back on the land that I loved, even if I knew it couldn't be forever, and I spent as much time as I could out exploring. No textbook could ever capture the wonder I experienced and the knowledge I gained while discovering the beauties of Amburla riding my new mare, Shannon, who I'd just recently broken in. I was developing a good eye for horses, but something must've been guiding my hand the day I picked Shannon from a mob of wild horses I'd brought in to refresh our mounts. Shannon became the best little horse I ever owned, and the two of us formed a partnership I've never found with another horse since.

We worked a lot of long hours together, dragging hot days that she never complained about, as fresh at the last moment of the job as she'd been wide-eyed and ready to roll at saddling up pre-dawn.

She was an extremely intelligent, liver-chestnut quarter horse with a light mane and tail. Shannon and I were best mates and we went all over Amburla together.

How lucky I'd feel riding her through that rugged landscape of reds, greys and muted greens stretching away to the walls of the MacDonnells, beneath a desert sun so sharp it had no colour, except in the brilliant blue of the Outback sky framing some of the most spectacular landforms on earth.

The MacDonnell Ranges change colours throughout the day, as the sunlight changes direction – orange, red, purple, blue-grey. Stare as you like, ride, drive or fly to the same spot every day for a year, and you'll never see the same thing twice.

Made up of bare quartzite and several layers of different sandstones that stretch about 380 kilometres east to west, the ranges contain mysteries and secrets still hidden after thousands of years of indigenous inhabitants and the last two hundred or so of Western-tradition science.

It's a magic place with flora and fauna unlike anywhere else – the Territory, Australia or the world. When I went out exploring, I'd give Shannon her head, letting her steer our path where she liked. We'd travel through rocky gorges where noisy flocks of mulga parrots flew overhead, their calls echoing off the ranges as they swept past us in search of food.

From a distance, the forbidding crags and dusty walls of the

ranges suggest they're nothing more than a continuation of
the harsh dry landscape surrounding them. But the western
MacDonnell Ranges have a wealth of unexpected gorges and
waterholes that are like small oases and are a lifeline for plants
and animals.

Cycads, plants that look like New Guinea natives' feathered
headdresses, grow against the rock walls. They are in fact survivors of a time when the MacDonnell region had weather
closer to that of New Guinea today – wet, lush and hot. Ghost
gums, pale and spindly, hook themselves onto almost vertical
cliff faces to capture the water and sunlight they need to
survive.

There are actually over 600 plant species in the Mac-
Donnells – twenty species of spinifex alone – including grasses,
herbs and trees, like ruby saltbushes, witchetty bushes, mallee,
mulga, cassias with perfumed yellow flowers, whitewoods,
bloodwoods, and white cypress pines.

To survive there they need that great touchstone of all life
on earth – water – but they also need to be very adaptable.
River red gums, for instance, actually shed limbs – just drop
them off – when the water supply is low, so that the main part
of the tree can keep alive. While out on the flat country the
mulga trees' leaves and branches funnel water down their
trunks to quickly reach the ground and their roots below,
moving it efficiently away from the evaporating heat above the
surface.

The survival techniques of the plants, trees and animals,
evolved over millions of years, constantly reminded me just
how determined Nature can be to hang on to any spark of life
in her creations. Some wildflowers, like the mini daisies,
germinate and quickly flower after a few days of rain from seeds

that have lain dormant in the ground for months, sometime years. They spring back to life, just like that little frog that got me into so much trouble at school.

But whatever the trick of survival may be, it's water that contains and sustains life. The MacDonnells are the best-watered district in central Australia, and the main river, the Finke, is confidently reckoned by many experts to be the oldest watercourse on earth.

I can never get over why people call Outback Australia the Dead Heart. It may not be the easiest place in the world to live, but millions of creatures and plants do it. People here don't have the smoothest run of things with the extremes of the environment, the cold at night, the searing heat of the day, and the sheer distance between watering holes, but those of us who call the place home can't imagine living anywhere else.

Beautiful country like the MacDonnells deserves our respect, and riding through there on Shannon, I felt respect for all the creatures that survived there and awe at the wonder of the place. Shannon and I would get a good workout cantering for a couple of kilometres. Then we'd make our way up the river bank and over a steep little hill before the 10-kilometre stretch home.

On reaching the top of the hill I'd take a breather and give my cherished friend a short rest. From there I could look out to Mount Zeil, the highest peak in the Northern Territory at under 1300 metres. It's a dwarf compared to what the area could manage millions of years ago, I'm told. Geologists say that millions of years ago, forces folding and pushing created mountain ranges in that part of the world at least as high as today's highest, the Himalayas. But the Himalayas, and Everest, their crowning peak, are a mere 60 million years old.

Often, I'd find fossilised sea shells. In another ancient time, this landscape was submerged beneath a vast inland sea. It was covered by ice sheets during the Ice Age. Then, just recently, around 300 million years ago, the blueprints for the rivers and the canyons – features we now know as Kings Canyon or Glen Helen Gorge – as well as the MacDonnell Ranges themselves, were laid down. Two hundred million years later a time traveller from today would have roughly recognised the area, if he took a look at them, say, 65 million years ago. For those mighty ranges have been slowly eroded, by wind and water, to become the relative foothills they are today. Sand gradually changed to rock, the inland sea shrank, becoming shallower and shallower, till all the water evaporated leaving nothing but a crust of salt and millions of fossils to mark its ever having been there.

But it was that same achingly slow process of erosion that created the tucked-away canyons, gorges, caves and waterholes that make the MacDonnells today an ark of fascinating plant life and hypnotic geology. Whereas, the Himalayas, I'd think, they're just covered in snow and not much else, aren't they?

The MacDonnells contain yesterdays further back than anywhere else you'd like to name, todays as startlingly beautiful as you can see and tomorrows that promise a future as intricate and unknowable as survival is anywhere – all evidence of the variety, mystery, and tenacity of life.

Painters like Albert Namatjira as well as photographers and film makers have come out here to try and capture some of the magic diversity of the place. It's almost impossible not to do a good job, either: the sheer beauty of the area does most of the artists' work for them.

But, good as paintings and photographs might get, you have

to be there to discover that, just when you figure you've seen it all, a minute later, you'll have your socks knocked off by another startling view.

And I lived there. I still do. If that's not a privilege I don't respect just about every day of my life, you might as well stop reading this book right here. Because if the story of my life has been nothing else, it's been about how living in Central Australia has opened my eyes to the reality of surviving in this world.

So now a dream was starting to grow in my own heart. Perhaps it came out of those three months when I was out on my own most of the time on the bore runs. But after travelling and exploring the close to half a million hectares of Amburla, through country that most Australians would never see outside of books or television, I knew that if people couldn't get out here themselves, I wanted to somehow bring the real Outback to them, to do something that truly captured the magic and beauty that surrounded me every day of my life.

Something else had got to me too. It was around that time that Mel Gibson was making a name for himself in the Mad Max movies. The films showed the world the Australian Outback, too, and the combination of Mel's acting and the background really clicked with me.

Enough to go to my dad and tell him that I wanted to go to Sydney to acting school and put my own stamp on big screen adventures in the Outback. Dad stood there quietly, scratched his head, looked at me, and asked me what I thought would make me stand out from the mob who probably had the same ideas I had.

'I'm different,' I said.

Not much argument about that, Dad said, but he also reminded me that I'd done a deal with him that I could leave school after year ten if I did a trade. He reckoned that, right then, I was fifteen years old, four years training in mechanics would see me to nineteen, and then I'd still be young enough to follow my dreams, whatever they were then.

Like parents everywhere Mum and Dad valued a qualification as a safety net in life. But they didn't ever try to shoot me down in flames, either. They knew I loved the country and they knew there was a fair bit of get up and go in me that even the wide Outback mightn't be big enough to hold in on its own, especially if I was talking about acting and films, which reach every corner of the world. So they supported me in my thinking, but always put up the other side of the question, so that I could see more than one point of view, so I could come to a well-balanced decision.

Dad's main point, my age, was the clincher, of course. There'd be years ahead for plans to entertain the world with the beauty and excitement of Outback Australia. And just as importantly, studying a trade would give me time to actually work out how to put those dreams into some sort of shape. I know one thing: if fifteen-year-old Troy Dann had landed in Sydney with a swag on his back and not much more to show for himself, there was every chance he wouldn't have got anywhere as far down that bulldust track to the dreams I have since. Let alone the ones now close enough to reach, with enough real-life experience to know where to grab hold of them.

A lot of that experience would come from studying and applying my trade. Knowing what I knew when I finished, just like Dad had told me, there weren't too many blokes who could pull the wool over my eyes. But that was ahead of me, and right now there were four years of hands-on study to do.

CHAPTER 11

....

THE DIESEL MECHANIC APPRENTICE

I applied for two places: Transport and Works with the government, and McMahons Construction. The government position would have been a routine nine-to-five, five-days-a-week job, but luckily I didn't get it. Instead, McMahons took me on, and that was a completely different story.

With McMahons I ended up travelling all over the Territory to road construction jobs as far out as the Queensland, South Australian and Western Australian borders.

But for the first two years of my apprenticeship the job was in Alice Springs, working on machinery brought back in after breaking down on any of the sites dotted around the Territory. Normally, there'd be two first-year apprentices, but I was on my own that year, with two in their second year, one in his third, and two in their fourth year above me.

Just as apprentice stockmen have to ride at the back of

the mob, first years at McMahons had the dirty jobs. First up on a Monday was sweeping out and cleaning up the big shed with its twelve inside and outside work bays. Sweeping is straightforward enough, but cleaning up oil and grease spills really gets you down and dirty. With just the one first-year apprentice – me – cleaning could take all Monday and into Tuesday before I actually got my hands dirty learning the real part of the job.

I was on clean-up right through first and some of second year, when the new apprentices were off at trade school or whatever. It was really only in third year that I got to spend most of my time working on machinery, but by then I knew every part of an engine that could spring a leak or spill out greasy waste.

I'd expected I'd go straight in and start working on machines from day one, but it was important to know the whole job from the ground up. I've since learned that you find out more about how things work by cleaning up after them on the times they haven't. What you should have just learned doing the dirty stuff is how to avoid the cleaning up by getting the job done right in the first place.

Around this time, my eyes were opening up to another world as well. I already had a fair idea of how it worked, because it's difficult for anyone raised on the land to miss how the whole males and females thing operated. Practically. But, like most people, for me the theory didn't kick in until puberty, and it seemed like the most topsy-turvy theory of all, the idea that you can feel someone is so special to you that nothing else in the world matters.

I was just fifteen, in my first year as an apprentice, when I first discovered how being in love could turn everything you took for granted about life, the world and yourself, inside out, upside down, up in the air and down in the dumps all in one. And then, a second later . . .

It happened one night, when I was out with some mates. It was my turn to shout, so I went to the bar. Standing there, turning out my pockets for change, a dollar coin dropped to my feet. As I bent down to pick it up, another hand got there first. This hand very kindly wiped the coin on my light beige jeans before returning it. It left a small mark on my pants, but as I looked up from that hand to the smiling face of its owner, I reckoned this meeting was worth the laundry bill.

An idea had already formed about that. 'You'll have to clean those now,' I said.

'Oh, will I?' she replied, cheeky as all get out.

For the rest of the night, the two of us kept bumping into each other in that crowded room. I'd seen it happening when I was younger: one night my governess and a helicopter pilot circled one another at the home station for hours before ending up giggling and laughing in the room next to mine right through to the next morning. But it's a whole different ball game when you're a player, not a spectator.

I found out her name was Sarah, and also where she lived. So I took my jeans around a few weeks later, knocking on the door with my heart in my mouth. She opened it, grinned broadly, and my heart thumped back into my chest.

'Here they are, then,' I said, holding out my jeans, the coin's stain upppermost on them.

'You're serious?' she said.

Well, serious is as serious sees, because by the grins on our faces some passerby might have thought we were auditioning for clown school.

That little ploy to give me good reason to drop around and see Sarah again worked. On top of that, she did clean my jeans for me, which I ended up in two minds about, because that small mark on my pants was where we'd first touched.

The way we started off was the way things went with Sarah and me. We always had a lot of fun together, and for the next four years Sarah and I were an item, even during long periods of separation in the last two years of my apprenticeship, when I was out working in bush camps. Or when I was in Darwin for two months each year for the first three years, studying the theory side of the trade at the university there.

I had a lot of fun in Darwin. One such time was when I was about sixteen years old. Another student and I went off at lunch time to take a look at some of Darwin's beaches.

We started to walk along a beach, but my mate told me it was a nudist beach so we had to take our clothes off. When in Rome ... So off came the clobber, and on we went. Sure enough, everyone on the sand and in the water was dressed in sunshine and fresh air, nothing but, and some of the ladies (not that I was looking), were well worth the sunlight spread over them, too.

I went in for a swim, came out and, you guessed it, my mate had disappeared and my clothes with him. All of a sudden I was a shy kid from the country. So I walked up to the car park, making out all the way I was as comfortable buck naked as a fish in a pond. Which was fine as long as everyone around me was 'dressed' the same way. But the people in the car park were all fully clothed, so I was the odd man out, so to speak.

There was my mate, sitting in the car, windows wound up, laughing himself silly while I tried to keep myself a little conservative as I knocked on the window yelling at him for my clothes.

Finally he let me into the car. I got dressed and was back to the college in time for afternoon classes. But I never fully trusted that bloke again.

Another time, when I was eighteen and still with Sarah, I was in Darwin but had the weekend off. By then I had a two-door Monaro HJ coupe, a real street machine, that I'd put a lot of time and care into. I thought I was too cool in that car, and I should have been, after the thousands of dollars I spent on it. I could do up to 240 kilometres an hour in it red-lining, and blow off most of my mates' WB utilities, which would top out at around 205.

On this weekend I wanted to see Sarah, so a quick trip down to Alice Springs was the plan of the day – and the night. A mate offered to go with me to give me a spell from driving, so I could go non-stop. Darwin to Alice is roughly 1500 kilometres, and a lot of the trip is on roads with an open speed limit, like most roads in the Territory.

We left at eight o'clock on Friday evening. Tearing down the highway at around 200 clicks per, we were making really good time. We'd been maybe two and a half hours and were just south of Katherine when we came upon a road detour where another company were working on the road.

Bugger it, I thought. I'll get on the new graded section and have the road to myself.

It was a moonlit night, which was lucky, because the mob who did the road work put their drainage culverts in using the reverse method to McMahons. We'd put them in first, then build the road around them. Not this mob.

So, I was hooning along at about 149 kilometres per hour

when I saw a big black nothingness 400 metres or so ahead of me. I hit the brakes, slid sideways and ended up, I promise you, true as true gets, just centimetres from the edge of a 20-metre-wide, 5-metre-deep hole that would have swallowed the Monaro, mate and me without even noticing.

Back on the main part of the road, things settled back to something approaching normal, apart from the kangaroo hopping the car was doing due to the nerves in my legs jumping as I tried to work the pedals.

We pushed on, but my mate was getting toey, wanting to drive. I know I'd taken him on as a back-up driver, but it was my car, right? My car.

Still, it was four in the morning, I'd been at the wheel eight hours straight, had almost killed myself and had damaged my paintwork. Maybe I wasn't thinking as straight as I should've been. This love thing could be the death of me – or more likely the speeds I was doing could be. Or maybe I figured Sarah deserved a little bit of energy in me when I got there.

It was to be a surprise, you see. I was planning to get to Sarah's place around six on Saturday morning, before she had to head off to a half-day's work starting at eight. It was really important to me, love-crazy as I was, to hit that magic 6 a.m. mark and have at least an hour with Sarah before she got ready for work.

So, against every instinct a Monaro driver has in him, I handed over the wheel. I wasn't comfortable sitting in the passenger seat, especially watching the speedo up around the 200 mark, because it looked a whole lot different from that angle. But I was tired, and the jangle had set in from missing that bog-old hole back there, and I finally managed to nod off.

Two seconds, three, bang. The word 'Detour' smacked up

across the bonnet of the car, attached to a sign that my mate had hit at the full 200, missing the road's turn. We slid sideways again, right off the bitumen, and did a tyre while we were at it. Luckily, we weren't hurt, but I might have wished some damage on him if I'd seen what daylight eventually revealed about the condition of my car.

I fixed the tyre, put the wheel in the back and powered on, finally clocking ten hours for the whole trip's 1500 kilometres, which I think back on now with a mixture of pride and wonderment at my stupidity and the powers of testosterone!

But I got to Sarah's at six, knocked on her open window, had the sort of reunion eighteen year olds reckon is the only sort going, then spent the weekend after she'd finished work with her. I actually had to start the drive back mid-Sunday morning, so the time was short, but love makes you do crazy things, and I wouldn't trade the memory for a garage full of Monaros. Certainly not Monaros that looked like mine did after my mate's run-in with the detour sign.

Without that Monaro Sarah and I might have never seen each other. Once, I was out working with Dad back at Amburla on a holiday break from McMahons. We were contract mustering, and would finish loading the cattle under floodlights onto trucks at nine or ten in the evening. Then I'd race into town to see Sarah, before heading back out for a 5 a.m. start. I managed this for two days without trouble. But on the third morning, when I was halfway back from town sometime before five in the morning, I fell asleep at the wheel while I was doing 160.

My eyes flicked open to see the tacho registering 130, but I was going backwards! If you've ever been in a situation like this, you'll know that the brain seems to take forever to actually figure out what's going on. Something – instinct, luck, I don't know – told me to just touch the brake pedal lightly, and not to stamp hard to try to come to a sudden stop. I gave it a delicate touch, and heaven smiled down on me. The car spun through 180 degrees, and there I was back on the bitumen, heading in the right direction, doing 110, all in one piece, and trying to work out whether I was just plain bad or whether there was something wrong with me.

I made it back to the job at hand, eyes wide as golfballs the whole way. But when I got back to the station, I had no time to worry about what might have been.

CHAPTER 12

OUT ON THE ROAD

The best thing about the four years with McMahons was that, in the last two years, I travelled all over the Territory, so I saw even more of the country than I had moving around with the family.

That was the bonus. Of course, those years between the ages of fifteen and nineteen are most important in terms of character building. And all the time I was learning my trade and applying it on the job, I was also learning a whole lot about human beings and the way we live our lives. I realised that the old equation of responsibility and danger went together every minute of the working day, however long those days were and however weary I got. My job was to stay on top of whatever task was at hand and to give the job 100 per cent of my attention because, without it, danger could enter the equation. There'd be time enough later to kick up my heels, let my hair down and get up to whatever fun and games time off might bring.

My job description was Diesel Fitter, which meant I got to work on all the big machines working out there, wherever they were: the border, the Petermann Ranges, Uluru (Ayers Rock). I had to fix all the heavy earth-moving equipment – bulldozers, graders, scrapers, front-end loaders – so I got to work a lot of hot oily metal on wheels or tracks.

But, lift my eyes, or take a smoko break, and there I was, in my idea of Paradise. Red earth, hardy vegetation, sky so blue you figured someone was trying to sell it to you with a quick touch up to fool the eager customer.

As usual, look a little closer and that wide, arid land was teeming with life, especially where the road works turned soil so that insects and ants had to scurry about rebuilding their nests. Big and important as our machines and our job might have been linking the scattered outposts of human life out here via roads, right at ground level the tiny survivors of millions of years of harsh conditions were just getting on with what had been hard-wired into them – the business of survival. In fact, when you looked at it more closely, the job all those insects and ants were doing was not all that different from mine. They were working to keep them and their kind together, getting by, surviving, making sure they'd still be there tomorrow. Yet, as far as I could see, those little fellas had never come up with the idea of smoko. They just kept going and going.

My four years' apprenticeship shaped a lot of my life after-wards, and in some ways much of that was down to the example shown me by those little creatures, that the job's always there to be done and persevering gets you through. Lucky for human beings, the job isn't the same, day in, day out – there's a bit of variety in our existence. But the same rule applies. Throw in the towel and you've just wasted everything you put in to get where you are.

Working out of town on jobs meant staying in bush camps. I was right at home out there, of course, unlike a lot of the other blokes, who got hungry to get back into town pretty quickly.

During those last two years of my apprenticeship I pretty much lived in the camps fulltime, with up to fifty or sixty other blokes. There might be two or three women out there – the foreman's wife or girlfriend, or whoever was in charge of the cooking – but otherwise it was an all-male life in the middle of what other people might call nowhere.

Some blokes were still working on the roads ten or twenty years after they'd walked into their first camp as an apprentice. That might have suited them, but I had different ideas. They didn't get in the way of my doing the job I was being paid to do, but what others might be complaining about – the isolation – was just icing on the cake to me.

The chance to get out in my free time into the surrounding countryside was the highlight of every place I worked. Because, while some people couldn't see any difference between one place and another, to my eyes every place was unique.

I'd been five months on the job at the new Barkly Homestead Roadhouse 500 kilometres north of Alice Springs, in flat, black-soil, open-plains country with not a tree for miles, working my butt off with everyone else to get the place ready for the next tourist season.

We were all looking forward to the big party on opening night in the new roadhouse, celebrating a job well done. But on that very afternoon the boss called me over and told me to pack my bags for the truck heading out to another job up at

Churchills Head, north of Tennant Creek. I was devastated to be missing out on the big night, but that was the way it went out there – always another job that needed doing yesterday a little further up the track.

The boss knew I was at home in the bush, and would give my all to the job, even so far as volunteering to do a double shift, working day and night a lot of the times.

Night shifts had their particular attractions, for want of a better word, at Churchills Head. The site we were working was well known as a haven for snakes, particularly black-headed pythons, which were attracted to the work area after dark by the vibrations of the heavy rollers through the earth and the lights on all the machinery. It was nothing to drive along the access track and see seven or eight snakes sliding their way towards all the action.

I used to collect snakes back then, and had an old tea chest in my room with a whole mob of pythons in it. It was known around the camp, so when a mate of mine called Ralph found a little beauty out there he thought nothing of bringing it in and putting it in the tea chest. At breakfast he told me there was a new tenant in there waiting for me.

I went into my room, reached straight down into the chest, and *whack*, the snake leapt up on to my arm. I pulled my hand out reflexively, but the snake kept coming, fangs out and spitting mad, ending up a centimetre from my nose. My eyes were crossed staring at it, but luckily I had enough of a grip to stop it short of sinking those fangs into me. I slowly put the creature back in the tea chest, sat down to calm my pounding heart and checked my snake guide book.

Ralph had brought me something that *looked* like a black-headed python. But in the juvenile stage, one of Australia's most venomous reptiles, the western brown, can pass for a blackie.

A fangin' angry western brown just off the tip of my nose was close enough for me. I decided it might be time I returned my whole collection to the bush. So the tea chest went out with me on the next shift, and all my flat-bellied mates got their tickets back into the wild.

Maybe Ralph ('Snake-man', I should call him) knew that Blackie was really Brownie and he was just having a joke. He sure was always a comic sort of bloke. But he had a way with words when it came to the ladies.

Once Ralph and I stopped in for lunch at a local roadhouse, the Hiway Inn, and got to talking to a couple of attractive English backpackers.

Ralph's job was to drive a 30-tonne roller. Those machines don't take a lot of brains, because all a driver has to do is guide the machine back and forth, back and forth, all day, crushing down the road surface with sheer weight alone.

The girls asked me what I did for a living, so I answered: 'Diesel mechanic.' The grease on my overalls was enough of a giveaway of that.

Then they asked Ralph.

'Final Trim Compaction Engineer,' he said. I'd never heard roller driving sound so technical and impressive! Still, the gift of the gab can take you a long way, though I know it never pays to ask a roller driver about his love life — it's sure to be flat-out lies.

I should know, I had a stint at it myself, and it nearly put an end to more than just my love life. The foreman from Alice Springs had come in to collect a 30-tonne roller we'd been using that had broken down. The brakes were gone and the engine had a habit of turning itself off. This great brute of a machine was sitting at the top of a hill 3 kilometres away from the work camp, where an even bigger machine was waiting to transport it to the next job in Katherine via the workshop.

Nobody wanted to drive the thing, because we all knew its little problems, and there was no time to fix it, so I put my hand up, the old spring action going in my shoulder that's got me into more trouble over the years than I like to think of. Everyone else was happy because the machine was going to end up at the bottom of the hill in one piece (hopefully), and because they weren't going to have to get it there!

I got up on the roller, turned the engine over using a screwdriver on the solenoid on the starter motor and started rolling her down a long, banked-up slope towards the camp. A mate of mine, Tassie, was driving a service truck. He reckoned he'd stick close and do whatever he could to slow me down if I got into trouble. I looked at his little truck then down at the 30 tonnes I was sitting on and told him to enjoy the country drive, so much use he'd be. But I was glad to have him with me.

We got over the crest of the slope, and it was all downhill from there. If it went over and took me with it, goodnight sweetheart. Then the engine cut out on me, taking the power steering with it. Suddenly I had no control, none, over this huge machine that slowly but surely was edging its way towards one side of the slope. I left the steering wheel, ran down to the motor, and got the screwdriver onto the solenoid again. Tassie, white-faced in the service truck, was still driving nearby, but not so close that he'd go over the edge with me — he wasn't that stupid.

Cranking the engine madly I finally got it fired up again. I

raced back to the wheel and guided the roller back out towards
the crown of the slope. Which meant I was at just the right
angle for the next potential disaster to hit. The engine failed
again and I was heading for the bank on the other side. It was
like someone in the sky was asking, 'Do you want to be
crushed to death left side first, or right?

Tassie decided he'd be my brakes, and he swung the service
truck in front of me, and let the roller butt up against its rear.
But all that was doing was damaging the back of the truck
every time the roller banged up against it. It sure wasn't
slowing the roller down. I waved him away in the end, because
if things had gone just a little wrong the roller would've gone
right over him and the truck, and all we'd have found in that
flattened mess would have been a 'map' of Tassie.

I reckon it was that same someone in the sky who, when
I used the screwdriver trick the third time, kicked the engine
over again for me, cracking the bleeder screw on the fuel
pump. I was back in the driver's seat, with the roller lined up
straight for the camp, two and a half clicks away a minute later,
so I figured the best option was to put the gears into neutral.
With the brakes shot I had no control over speed, but at least
the steering mightn't lock up on me with no load on the
engine.

The roller gathered speed all the way down the slope,
30 or 40 kilometres per hour, faster and faster, 30 tonnes of
machinery, till she must have been going 80 clicks rolling free.
If the motor cut again I was going westward and there'd be
no time to get her started again. I was in the lap of the gods
and I shot past Tassie with my fists in the air (I thought if I
was going down I may as well do it in style).

Finally I rolled to a halt, landing safely at the bottom of

that terrible descent. It'd had just enough momentum from the bottom of the slope to get to the work camp, and it rolled the whole way there to the loading ramp!

There was relief all round and laughter on faces that hadn't any blood in them ten minutes before. So the roller was loaded up and moved on to the next job, and as far as I know, once she came out of the workshop, she never caused that sort of trouble again.

❖   ❖   ❖

One of the first tests of my trade and one of my proudest moments was when I took over fixing a front-loader that no one else had been able to sort out. It had a steering problem so that, turn left, it went right.

I figured it was most likely a hydraulics problem, so I got in at the base of the steering column, took out the valve body and went back with the lot to the workshop to take it apart. Nuts, bolts, springs everywhere and me with the manual trying to sort the jigsaw out. I spotted one of the springs had weakened, allowing oil to flow both ways through a valve that should have only let it go in one direction. That explained why the steering went its own way half the time. It virtually 'responded' on a random 50–50 fall of the coin as the oil flow chose which way it would go. I replaced the spring, put the whole box and dice back together, set it back into the machine – and she was sweet thereafter. From then on some of the major problems were thrown my way, and I liked nothing more than a good challenge.

❖   ❖   ❖

I continued to work at Churchills Head, and soon I'd worked

eight months, including the five months on the Barkly Tableland, without a day off. I was about eighteen, going on nineteen, and I was getting fairly tired, putting in over 100-hour weeks.

A change is as good as a holiday, someone must've thought, because I was sent to work on the gas pipeline at Katherine. I was in the last stage of my four-year apprenticeship, but already I was being treated like a full tradesman, to the extent that I'd been put in charge of the clearance crew on the job. We cleared the ground ahead for the pipes to be laid, so we were always a little in front of the main action.

There were 150 men and something like a hundred machines on that job, so it was the biggest I'd worked on till then, especially because there were only five mechanics to service all those machines. It was obvious there were going to be problems keeping up with the backlog of breakdowns, problems it would be easiest to blame us for when they started to mount up. All of which led to my first encounter with the unions.

There's always been a lot of talk about unions around Australia: the fors and against, whether they were the best or the worst thing that ever happened to the country, with never much middle ground between the two positions.

Out on these big, widespread road jobs the workers would often pass through as many as ten gates on private property to get from site to site. Some blokes were employed to do not much else all day but open and close gates, sitting beside 'their' gate and lifting a finger about ten or twelve times a day for big dollars. For someone who'd grown up on a property where everyone mucked in and pulled their weight for the job at hand, regardless, I reckoned this was out and out waste.

I wasn't big on the whole union idea, and neither Tassie

nor I had joined. Then the union called a strike for extra washing facilities – a couple of machines to keep the work clothes clean. This strike was set for the same day shift before the night that a disco was on in Katherine.

For once Tassie and I were close enough to a town to have a party, and the day-shift strike meant all the work we'd planned to do to be free that night would be put back. We wouldn't be able to go anywhere with the worksheet not cleared of jobs.

After eight months straight, right or wrong, nothing was going to stop me getting into that disco and letting my hair down on the dance floor. So I started on the job I had – a full shift in it for sure – replacing the head on a big old Caterpillar motor, when a four-wheel-drive drove up and a couple of union reps hopped out.

They started going on to me about there being a strike on and that I was letting down the side, and to down tools now or I'd know about it. I let them know a few things, too, about the hours Tassie and I were working, with little time off in the past eight months, not the regular two weeks on, two weeks off with full pay the union members were getting.

Then one of them moved forward as if he was going to pull me down from the machine, so I just shoved him back, forgetting about the 18-inch shifter I had in my hand. Both he and his mate decided discretion was the better part of valour, and they got back into their vehicle and shot through. Spilt milk, so I shrugged and got on with the job.

But when I went back to the main camp site later I saw the foreman and told him what had happened. We had a bit of a grin, because he'd made out he wasn't working till they were out of sight himself.

Tassie and I went into town, had a really good night at the

disco, and got back to the camp at about four in the morning.

At seven o'clock there was a knock on my door, and my top mate, Spog, my boss, another mechanic, was standing there, saying I have to get myself down to the foreman's office because I've got myself into a spot of trouble.

There I was with three months of my apprenticeship left to do, and it looked like they were about to turf me out without my trade qualification. I walked in and the foreman was there with a company executive. They asked what happened.

Well, I told them fair and square my side of things. How it had all come about because of the unbroken hours I'd been working at three sites in a row. About having to leave Barkly Homestead the very day the finishing party was on, no two weeks on two weeks off for me, all of which was fair enough while I was putting my hand up to do extra work, but a bit rough when I'm being dragged over the coals about a couple of washing machines. The two blokes heard me out, then made me wait outside the office while they had a private chat.

It was ten minutes of my life I could have done without, as I sat there thinking how such small things can bring the biggest plans and the hardest work unstuck, and what would I say to Mum and Dad, how disappointed they'd be.

Finally, the foreman and the other bloke came back and delivered their sentence: four days in Darwin at company expense in a five-star hotel!

So there I was heading for Darwin with $18,000 in the bank after eight months of hard slog. It sounded good and looked good, but when I sat down and worked out the figures, I discovered that I was netting two dollars when I worked fifteen to twenty hours on a Sunday because of the amount of tax I was paying. In my biggest week I grossed $3400, but 1800 of that went straight to tax. I was definitely no Kerry Packer.

It was pretty good money for a fourth-year apprentice on twelve dollars or so an hour. But it could have been better, with the bonus system that applied – to everyone but apprentices with a couple of months left in their training, that is. At the end of the job, the company terminated workers' contracts and paid a termination bonus, $5–10,000 worth. Because the job finished ahead of my apprenticeship, I wasn't 'terminated', so no bonus. You start to wonder how the world works some times, when you really look into things.

One thing I didn't look into while I was in Darwin was the bank balance dropping as I had the time of my life, to the tune of a thousand dollars a day over four days. There are probably still taxi drivers who remember the 100-per-cent tips they got from me that long weekend, or shop assistants who recall how I spent up big on clothes, shoes and other things I hadn't seen new for almost a year of working in overalls and workboots.

I reckon the extra hours I put into that apprenticeship at McMahons would have totalled six years of work experience in the four I spent with them, but I don't begrudge a minute of it, because I came out a fair mechanic. On top of that I'd been all around the Territory, and I'd seen places I've been back to since, and some I'll get out to again, as soon as the chance arises. Those places were full of characters, people who were such individuals the stories about them would take up three lifetimes! They were great years that stood me in good stead down the track, for all kinds of reasons, not least that I got to know even better the people and places of the Territory.

CHAPTER 13

MISTAKE CREEK

Finally my apprenticeship was finished! During the last few months I'd also been learning to fly. So when graduation day came, I had two qualifications under my belt: diesel mechanic and fixed-wing pilot.

I was offered a twelve-month contract working on the big mining machines up at Port Hedland for $60,000. It sounded pretty good to me, even more so when I decided that six months would be better. I could pick up thirty grand then spend the next six months driving around Australia learning more about the country.

This was the plan I had in my head when Dad rang. The station had been getting beaten around by a long stretch of drought. He asked me what my plans were, I told him, and then he said he could really use me at home. Well, I figured the work would always be there, but the chance to repay some of his faith in me was right now.

So I shelved the mining job, packed up my swag and headed for home. Now that I was qualified and had seen a bit of the working world, I did a deal with Dad: I'd work *with* him, not *for* him. I reckon it took him back a bit, me using those words, but I knew that, best mates as we were, if I started to think of him as my boss there was every chance we'd lose some of that feeling of working side by side that you take for granted when you're younger. Because when you're a kid you and your Dad are just out there doing it together. But if you're working 'for' someone – taking a wage and always deferring to the boss because he's the paymaster – that's the quickest way to throw a spanner in the works when two blokes are both fiercely independent, can't help but be because they're of the same flesh and blood.

I'd seen a lot of families fall apart with sons taking a pay packet till they were forty-something, always giving way to their dad and passing over innovations and different ways of doing things because the old man was set in his ways and he was the boss. By the time the son did take over, he was just as likely a father of adult boys himself, and the whole cycle might repeat itself until someone decided to chuck it in and walk away. Properties would pass out of family hands because the family had splintered, and there's nothing I hate to see more than traditions that have every reason to be strong, generation after generation, dying away.

The funny thing about tradition on the land and working the land is that it actually depends on innovation – responding to changing conditions, understanding the market you're providing raw material to and understanding that you have to react to what the buyers want, not what you've always done. You'll find that the people who have been on a place the longest and have established roots so deep it's like the place wouldn't be there if they weren't on it, they're the people most responsive to fresh challenges and new solutions to age-old problems.

It's always struck me as funny that a part of the country considered to be so dyed in the wool conservative and traditional as rural Australia is right out front when it comes to progress and innovations that, long term, benefit the whole country, everyone in the city as much as those of us so far out pollution is a three-syllable word.

In my case I was lucky enough to have a father who always thought, and continues to think, about how to improve work methods, every-day efficiency and long-term productivity. So I knew that we weren't likely to argue too much about the best way to move forward in overall terms. That just left two grown men working side by side on a day-to-day basis, and we'd been able to do that as long as I could remember. So this particular homecoming was a challenge I was looking forward to – partnership with my old man.

As it happened, Dad had just bought another property, called Mistake Creek, up on the Western Australian border. It was a beautiful block, running about 20,000 head of cattle with around 5000 head of donkeys on it. Three thousand head of camels rounded out the stock count. The property was close enough to the Argyle diamond mine for me to while away the hours when I was working hard digging holes for fences hoping that my crowbar would strike a huge deposit of diamond. No such luck, of course, but a lot of fencing went up with a little more enthusiasm for the work than usual.

On Mistake Creek it was a bit of a family affair. My older sister, Simone, worked the office, and my younger sister,

Tanya, packed the meat in the portable abattoir Dad had established. Mum was there teaching Heidi, my littlest sister, as well
as cooking for up to twenty staff.

When I first arrived I applied my trade to fixing the
machinery. The trade and experience with McMahons stood
me in good stead for that as well as for covering long distances.
To travel 1000 kilometres in a day was no mean feat – it's just
the way of the Outback! Gee I love that word.

There's hardly a manual skill that goes to waste in the
Outback – everything from plumbing to knitting, all sorts of
engine mechanics to midwifery – anyone who can put their
hands to good use will never find themselves idle out here.

You can't escape the sheer size of the place, so any skill
that allows you to tame that a little is worth its weight in
whatever you want to weigh it in. Independent air travel is
right up there, as far as I'm concerned, for getting some control
over the scale of the Outback.

I spent a lot of hours in the station's little Cessna 182Q
plane, a great little machine. Her call sign was Mike Lima Papa,
M.L.P., so I always called her 'My Little Plane', even though
she belonged to Mum and Dad. I chased a lot of cattle from
the air. A lot of it was low-level flying, naturally enough, and
there was a lot to think about with the ground sometimes only
metres below. In a plane, there's none of the flexibility of
helicopters, which can turn on a sixpence and hover in one
position.

You seem to spend more time flying past the centre of
activity in a fixed-wing plane than actually towards it, so the
trick is to learn to create the next situation on the ground.
You're actually trying to make the job for people on the
ground easier by the time you've flown by. In a sense, you're

always doing and leaving, doing and leaving. Whereas, in a chopper, you're in direct partnership with the stock camp on the ground every minute of the job.

Open country is easy, because you can get a mob moving and it's all straight lines. But if they get in under thick scrub, they start playing hide and seek with you. You can buzz them, but then you've buzzed right past. Whatever the animals are doing, you've always got to be paying attention to the wind. For instance, you avoid mustering downwind whenever you can, because if you try a sharp turn in strong gusty conditions, the wind can hit you so hard it's the ground that's hitting you next.

Those cattle might still be under the trees, though, so you buzz them and then do a wingover. This is something you start downwind, lifting the machine straight up and then into the wind, which forces a stall, so that you control your fall back to buzz them again. The second roar overhead, within 10 seconds or so, normally gets them moving again. But you can imagine what it's like with a really cunning beast: it will just stay under the trees, not budging, and there's not a thing you can do about it.

That's why I also love helicopters: you can virtually put them where you want.

When I wasn't mustering in the plane, I was flying on supply runs, checking fences, dams or bores, or just getting up in the air to save time in the day and to keep my skills sharp. I felt a real connection with the many pioneers of this part of the world, crossing it on foot, coming back by horse or camel or in carts and, in this century, motorised vehicles. But what they would have given to share the view that, until the aeroplane, only the wedge-tailed eagle and the other smaller birds of the region had all to themselves! I loved the freedom of kicking free from the ground and soaring through some of the most beautiful country on earth.

I've seen a lot of the Outback from the air, if someone asks me directions I often start describing landmarks way over the ground-level horizon, until I pull myself up and realise the person asking me is in a car.

❖   ❖   ❖

To help with the delivery of frozen beef and shifting of stock, I also qualified for my roadtrain driver's licence as I had to do a lot of driving while I was at Mistake Creek. Three-trailer roadtrains are the biggest road transport set-ups in the world: 150 metres of metal, rubber, dust and grease. The road's stretched out before you straight enough to fool a man from Mars that his grandfathers had been there before, and they leave a dust cloud behind that doesn't clear for an hour.

Those days were before the CD players and satellite-telephone link that drivers have now. Still, there was an air-conditioner and a cassette player, and I reckon my grandfather, who had to move on foot for a month or two as many cattle as roadtrains could truck in a day, would reckon we had it easy.

I'd transported meat from Mistake Creek. Dad had set up a portable abattoir on the station, with a staff of eighteen, plus a couple of stock camps. The portable abattoir cut down a lot of the expense that's involved when you're transporting cattle live from a place as far out as we were.

The road to Katherine from the station at Mistake Creek takes you through Top Springs, halfway between the tropics of Katherine and the open plains that stretch across to the

Western Australian border. I knew every inch of that road eventually.

I drove a White Road Boss, a beautiful truck with thirteen gears. I'd drive to Top Springs and meet another truck that would drive on to Melbourne. The truck freezer pan wasn't wide enough for the pallets so we couldn't use a forklift. Instead, I'd back the truck alongside the other and transfer up to 720 cartons, each about 30 kilograms, by hand. Nine times out of ten the other driver was elderly, so the job was all mine. Six hours it could take, without much more than a drink break here and there, and then the drive for home with a back on me that knew every kink in it was hard-earned.

There would be days on end driving, shifting cattle around from camp to camp or making trips up to Darwin with full loads and the road back waiting. I was on my own, like every other truck driver, so pretty much all that kept me going were legal 'shakers' – pills to keep you awake. I'm not proud of it now, but in those days, that's the way it was done. Lots of drivers did it for years and the same ones are probably still driving trucks today. But driving has its own responsibilities, and these days those pills are illegal and drivers often work in pairs so they can share the load. But it's definitely a different lifestyle to any other occupation I know. I salute you, truckie friends.

After hours and hours of driving, you could end up having hallucinations from exhaustion and from being too wired up from the shakers. It's another reason why, looking back, driving on those pills was dangerous and irresponsible.

One particular day I was driving along to the beat of Fleet-wood Mac, one of only two tapes I had and which I'd been listening to for four days straight after driving to Darwin, back to Mistake Creek, then out to Top Springs. There wasn't a lyric I didn't know and I knew which song came next when the last one was over. On the last leg for home, with a thermos of coffee and a few shakers in me to keep going, I drove over the crest of a hill into a huge mob of kangaroos.

They were bouncing and bobbing in front of me – I couldn't miss them. There were a couple up on the bonnet, kicking off as if they did circus stunts every day of their lives. And all without spilling a drop of blood. Yeah, every one of those roos had a can of Victoria Bitter beer in one hand, and big happy grins on their faces to go with it, too.

I pulled over to the side of the road, and the rampaging roos disappeared into thin air. A touch more coffee was in order but, that down the trap, I wasn't getting anywhere sitting there thinking about kangaroos' lousy taste in beer.

But now the roos were gone, and there were no empty cans of V.B. to clean up after them, so I started up the truck again and drove on. Fifteen kilometres down the track, I was suddenly in the middle of a nudist colony fun run. There were stark naked people laughing and smiling as they ran in front of the truck. I was starting to think it was all getting a bit funny, but with Mum and Dad away down in Alice Springs, I had to get home.

Well I didn't leave any dead nudists behind me as I drove straight through them, but my head still had another surprise in store. A great shed came out of nowhere right across the road. It was real enough, even if no one else could have seen it if they'd been there. I hit the semi brakes, the jake brakes, the trailer brakes – you name it, they were all on – and I pulled up by the roadside at a 20-degree angle!

Mistake Creek was starting to look further and further

away. The next morning's job of shifting cattle from one of the camps to the abattoir, something Dad and I had reckoned was critical before he left, seemed as much a pipe dream as this little drive had turned into. But I made it, crawling the last 10 kilometres home at 5 ks per hour, figuring that, as the hallucinations had a habit of racing up at me, no speed at all for two hours might fix it.

And so it was on to the next job. Talk about a jack-of-all-trades! As I've said before, there are so many things you have to be able to do yourself when you're running a station. You have to be a bit of a mechanic, a bit of an electrician, a bit of a plumber, a yard builder, stockman, fencer, earth-moving operator, veterinarian, hydraulics engineer, driller, builder, fireman, stud-biologist – the list goes on. It's still just like the old days, in that regard. Back then, it didn't matter whether people lived on a property or in a city, they were self-taught, handy and full of the good old Australian spirit, helping each other and not having to rely on handouts or some emergency service to do the job.

Earth moving was something I'd learnt about during my days with McMahons. On Mistake Creek we had an old Caterpillar D6C bulldozer. I'd always take my toolbox with me when I was working with her. Sometimes I was camping out for weeks on end, building or repairing the boundary fence lines and their flood gates or whatever else needed doing.

I'd be away from a roof and four walls sleeping in my trusty old swag, just as often on my own, but sometimes with one other bloke working the grader. He'd have to get used to me listening to old Slim or Charlie Pride, so it helped if he had an ear for good music or was deaf from the sound of machinery all day. Either way, not too many starlit nights went by without

the sound of guitars filtering through the crisp cold. When the
cassette finished the sounds of crickets or an owl hoot or a
howl of a dingo in the distance would put me to sleep, my
eyes still stinging from dust.

On one occasion, the next bloke I was expecting to see
was Dad, who was coming out to check how much more work
needed doing here, because the quicker it was done the
quicker I could get back to the stock camp for the next big
mob of cattle we'd planned to bring in.

This was ticking over in the back of my head: the old 'time
is money' mantra gets hold of you when you're a business-
person, whether your business is a corner store in the suburbs
or making a million wild hectares productive.

I'd bulldozed right up to the boundary 60 kilometres from
home, and had reached a really steep embankment. It must
have been around 15 metres down, way below, to Negri
River, which is the major river in the region. The embankment went both ways for kilometres, with the river and the
trees stepped along it, stretching away like a great glistening
snake skin across the landscape. My problem was, I had to be
on the other side of the dry river bed. Life never stops doing
that to you, does it? Wherever you are, maybe not right now,
but some time real soon, you have to get to the 'other side of
the river'.

Well, this was a case of right now, so I stood there looking
down, thinking that the old dozer on its tracks would take
forever if I decided to take it around the river to a crossing
spot 15 kilometres north. They don't exactly get up to a cracking pace, dozers, and if you push them too hard they'll shake
every tooth out of your head and half the nuts and bolts out
of themselves.

So, the immediate problem lay at my feet, and its solution was 15 metres below. The slope was on an angle of 70 degrees, gentle enough walking or sliding on your backside, but not something you'd want to take on with no way of stopping 16 tonnes of dozer. I figured that if I brought the machine gently up to the lip of the slope, and aimed for the first of the big old trees down there, I could slide down and then catch the tree with the blade of the dozer and slow myself down using my back rippers to dig into the earth. Then, shifting tree to tree, I could ease myself down to the river bed.

Easy as, standing up there on a bright sunny day with a week's work behind me, more ahead, and a problem that would make all that work so much tougher due to wasted time and unnecessary detouring.

I brought the dozer up to balance on the lip of the slope. There was no one around for kilometres, I reckon, but I tell you right now, if my mum had been there she would have probably given me a clip around the ear for even thinking about what I was about to do.

I was sitting in the dozer, which was balanced on the edge of the slope, when suddenly the great machine under me felt totally weightless, not a gram to it – or me either, for that matter. I looked around and I couldn't see anything but blue sky. The rest of the world had just gone out of view, and I felt like I was suspended inside a huge blue balloon that was lifting away, floating, taking me with it, higher and higher, to a place where nothing weighed anything. There were no sharp edges, no sudden stops and I had no sense of danger or of threats to life and limb.

And then the dozer tipped forward.

The sky just fell away from me, the blue streaking down

into green, white, rusty red, yellow and black, and the weight of the machine and of me rushed back in, right through the seat of my jeans. The jolting and the shuddering of my uncontrolled slide came thumping in, and the machine was pushed around sideways. My plan of catching the first tree head-on suddenly needed rethinking. But there was no time to think.

I lifted the rippers and locked my right clutch and brake pedal, trying to build in some resistance and move the machine back around so it was front on. But the slope was too steep and too short for me to get control in time. I skidded down, hit the tree side on, using it more like a brake, and then bounced off it and kept sliding, this time through another 90 degrees, so I was now going backwards. Well, the blue sky was back in front of my eyes, but I wasn't having too many dreamy thoughts of weightlessness and floating away. With all the noise and speed, the blue looked more like the blunt end of a huge great hammer powering down to hit me fair between the eyes.

My feet and hands were working the controls all the time, but the machine wasn't responding quickly enough – there was no way it could, I suppose, but that wasn't any reason to quit trying.

Bang, backwards into another tree, and with a bit of help from me, I spun around 180 degrees, still sliding, but forwards, so at least I could see the trouble I was about to land myself in. I ended up on the straight and level at the side of the river, no worse for wear, the machine pretty much the same, with the memory of a rollercoaster ride that real coaster fanatics would have given their eye teeth for.

I felt pretty happy with myself because some challenges just get to me and everything had worked, the plan had come off and Dad wouldn't know. I started climbing back up the slope to check out what I'd just managed. As I clambered up over the top lip I walked straight into Dad and George, another bloke who was working there with us. I should have known. Dad never misses a trick! It's the way of living on the land: blink your eyes and you'll miss something, so a good bushman is always alert to what's happening all around him.

'What the hell have you done? Where's the dozer?' Dad said.

I just nodded over the edge. 'Saved half a day, I reckon.'

He just lifted his eyes from the dozer sitting down there, and looked at me like I was six kinds of crazy working on seven.

'George, have a look at this,' Dad called out.

George took a look over the side. I watched his eyes following the marks down the slope where I'd bounced off one tree, caught the next and the next to where the dozer now was.

George laughed and so did Dad, but I could hear the relief in it as he looked to me.

'You're an idiot,' he said.

I took that as a compliment 'Times money,' I pointed out, proud of myself that things had worked out the way I'd figured they would.

In the end.

But there were still a few kilometres of dozing ahead of me to do. There was a race meeting at Timber Creek the next weekend, and with the minimum opportunities any of us had for a social life at Mistake Creek, the meeting was high on my list for the weekend.

Simone, Tanya and the governess from the property next to ours, a girl called Mandy, were going, so that promised a real turn-out by the local girls, another attraction for a twenty year old who'd just spent two months in the bush without any female company.

But the dozing work was priority one on Dad's books so, believe it or not, I missed that damn party.

CHAPTER 14

CROCS, COOLIBAHS AND CATS IN THE TOP END

Up close, with its coolibah trees and rubber bushes, the Top End is unmistakably Australian. Take the wide-angle view, though, with the creeks so long and wide and the country tabletop flat, and I can't help thinking of Hollywood westerns.

At Mistake Creek you'd swear you'd stepped up onto the big screen, sometimes, and you'd be expecting the next bloke you saw to be John Wayne.

In the Top End there are native creatures that I had never seen in the Centre: insects and birds by the millions, of course, but also many small marsupials that are quite different to their cousins further south in the arid desert areas. I loved getting out and about, spotting all these creatures that were half recognisable but still new to me.

One prehistoric creature native to the Top End I knew well enough from local legend and Territory-wide scare stories, but had never actually met before: the crocodile. Unlike central Australia, the Top End is full of waterholes and rivers to camp by, so showering at night often involved sharing the bath tub with freshwater crocs.

One memorable encounter with a croc was when we were out mustering cattle with a couple of new jackaroos who were with us for the first time.

'Jackaroo' has got around as a word you can use to describe any stockman, but it actually means blokes new to the trade who are still learning the ropes. Call an experienced stockman (a ringer) a 'jackaroo' and, depending on his mood, you might suddenly be seeing a starry sky dancing before your eyes in full daylight.

Anyway, we had two young fellas up from Tasmania, both fair haired, pale skinned and having never really been out in the bush. We had two or three thousand cattle loose in the bullock paddock, where a whole lot of the fences had been flattened by the last Big Wet. (Anyone who's never seen a real Top End thunderstorm should make it a life plan to get up here during storm season some time. The forces of all that huge sky-busting energy get right into you, and make you feel really small and about to burst both at once. The thunder and lightning send shivers up and down your spine as if your whole body is an antenna. It's hard to put into words, which is why the invitation stands to get yourself up here some time.)

The two watercourses that flow through the paddock – Mistake Creek itself and the Negri River – had flooded and pushed the fences out, making gaps we call 'flood gates', where the cattle can just walk straight out. Which is exactly why we were out there: to bring them back in and repair those fences.

The two young Tasmanians, my cousin Freddy Colson, another more experienced bloke, two helicopter pilots and I had pulled together about two and a half thousand head. We'd pushed them up a big creek, having to stay on our toes every inch of the way because a large number of the mob were feral. On top of that, a large percentage of them were bulls. Put the two together – that some of them weren't used to being worked to someone else's will plus all that cooped-up male energy – and the job needed total concentration.

I had the roos build big bonfires at two points in the dry river bed, where the fence had been destroyed. Those fires had to be kept going so that the mob didn't push back past us. If they did, we'd have to collect them all together again. I explained this to the new blokes, told them to each put their swag down beside the fire and make sure it stayed hot and high all night.

It was just about dusk, so I drove the old ute up to the fence we were heading for next day. There was no grid on the road, so Freddy was putting his swag down there to make sure the cattle didn't head through the unprotected opening.

It was about ten or eleven by the time I drove the four-wheel-drive towards the south-western end of the paddock, where there was a waterhole I planned to put my own swag beside. This way, there was a man at each point that the cattle could get out if they had a mind to.

I was feeling pretty happy with the arrangements, but I was thirsty. I hadn't had a drink for hours, and I was feeling as dry as the soles of my boots, with another half an hour to go before I reached the waterhole.

As luck would have it, there was a plastic cordial bottle that had shaken loose from under the passenger seat beside me. I grabbed that bottle and had the cap off and a mouthful-and-a-half of the liquid into me before I realised I was sculling clear brake fluid.

Well, anyone who's seen the job brake fluid can do when it's spilt on the paintwork of a car would know I was in trouble. My mouth was burning way down to my stomach, but there was nothing I could do, there was no other liquid I could put into me to dilute that fierce burning deep inside me.

I gunned the ute as fast as I could get the old motor turning over across the flat rocks that still lay between me and the waterhole, but it was fifteen minutes before I reached the water.

I leapt out of the vehicle and ran down to that water. With the headlights behind me lighting up the waterhole, I was down there and on to my knees with my head under the water in Olympics-competitive time, gargling water down my throat fast as possible. I swallowed it in, spat it out, swilled some more, swallowed and spat to get the taste out of my mouth and the fire from my belly for two, three minutes straight, nothing else in the whole wide world mattering a moment to me right then.

My mouth settled down some and I felt I could relax a little. The lights of the ute glittered yellow across the width of the waterhole. But suddenly I noticed there was something else glittering a whole lot closer. There were two red dots maybe half a metre in front of me, level with the water. Two red dots that it took me maybe two split seconds to realise were crocodile eyes.

I don't know what he'd been thinking while he just sat there not moving. It could be he was too puzzled by the strange behaviour of this ducking, diving, spitting, retching creature that had come visiting his private waterhole. Too puzzled to bite my head off, anyway.

And me? I wasn't thinking anything. Instead, I leapt back so far and so fast I reckon there should be an all-Australian event in the Olympics – the Backwards Crocodile Leap, with Troy Dann holding the record time. From the instant I was eyeball to eyeball with that croc to the moment I was standing back at the ute it was so quick the best electronic stopwatch going would have had trouble picking up the time.

I've seen a lot of crocodiles since, and I've seen what they can do to a full-size horse or cow unlucky enough to walk into their little feeding patch, and if I've got any cat blood in me that was one more life out of my nine gone into the debit column.

Next morning, I was out of my swag and into the ute at around 4.30 or so and driving back to pick up Freddy. My mouth was still a bit tender from the brake fluid, but it was coming back to normal. It was 6.30 a.m. by the time the sun hit the horizon and spread rays of light across the land to the cheer of the birds in the trees when the two of us returned to the creek to link up with our two Tassie jackaroos and a few stragglers.

But we caught them out. They were still asleep, their swags maybe 15 centimetres apart – forget the 50 metres I'd suggested – and the ashes of one fire, not two, were beside them.

The bellowing and the movement of the cattle during the night had spooked these tenderfoots too much to follow orders. As it turned out, there were some tracks of a couple of animals leading away, but we traced them and returned them to the main mob. So there was not too much damage done, but obviously the big scary scrubber bulls and the roof of the sky so high you can't reach the light switch when something goes bump in the night had put these two side by side for sleepybyes.

After a couple more months out there both blokes turned out pretty handy, but I could always get that pale southern skin of theirs burning blood red to the roots of their fair hair with the smallest reference to that night.

❖   ❖   ❖

As I said, some of the animals in the Top End I'd never seen in the Centre. I'll tell you a story that Dad flat out refuses to believe, but since it's here in black and white now . . .

I was out bringing in some horses for a muster, and was heading to what we called the horse paddock. Now, with everything the scale it is on Outback stations, the 'horse paddock' was actually a couple of square kilometres, bigger than a lot of people's entire farms closer to the eastern seaboard of Australia.

This particular paddock had really long grass after some good rains, and as far as you could see and in the mood I was in, everything was right with the world. I wasn't exactly reciting the best parts from A.B. Paterson poems or singing the collected hits of Slim Dusty, but that morning I was pretty happy with life and the whole damn thing.

To get where I was going I had to ride my bike past the bone dump, where all the refuse from our abattoir was dumped. I was sure I'd seen a big cat picking through that dump a couple of times. And this is where Dad has always tuned out, offering me a round-trip ticket to Loch Ness or Mount Everest if I was seeing monsters out there. But if you can't believe your own eyes, what can you believe? On the other hand, we've all seen things we have to look at twice to figure out, and we still get it wrong.

But there was no mistake this happy morning. It was a cat all right, and I'd spooked it away from breakfast in the bone dump. It bounded away through the grass, so I gunned my bike after it.

It was bouncing through the grass – now you see it, now you don't – except when I couldn't spot it, the shaking, slithering movement of the grass gave it away.

Now, we're not talking a tabby gone bush here. This was a cat like a leopard. Big, fast and dangerous.

There'd been a story about a couple of big cats escaping from a travelling circus in the west Kimberleys: stock had been found as well as a couple of horses with big raking claw marks on them. Some people reckoned crocs might have done it, because a croc can get as far as 20 kilometres away from water. But the marks were all wrong in those cases. It's just that most people, and quite rightly, nine times of ten, were looking for the most likely answer before they swung off into tales about escaped leopards.

But I know what I saw. It was no croc: it was quick and smart enough on its feet to change direction lightning fast, and it had that bouncing movement I've only ever seen when a big cat gets itself moving.

The cat got away from me, not that I can tell you even today what I would have done if I'd caught up with the thing. If it was what I'm sure it was, it might have been more a question of what it did to me!

It's times like that you wish you could just run your memories back through a videotape machine so that other people could see what you saw, instead of looking at you like you're setting them up for some punchline, or like you've had one too many for the road.

But there was no one else there with me, so that cat was just like the fish that got away. Which I guess is what the old croc I met in the waterhole says to his mates about me.

Aerial view of home – Amburla Brahman Stud, north of the Western MacDonnell Ranges.

The northern part of Amburla Station, showing the incredible contrasts in the country.

The southern range of Amburla near Mount Hay in a good season.

Dismantling a tank to transport to Amburla. Sometimes you have to be a jack-of-all-trades and master of none on the land.

My most favourite spot in the world: Mt Sonder near Glen Helen
in the Western MacDonnells, 30 kilometres from home.

Photo by Hans Boessem

A lonesome white gum tree surrounded by bush in the Western MacDonnells.

Photo by Hans Boessem

Brett, Tanya and me back in 1990 promoting fun in the Outback with
a few steps of our own.

Photo by Barry Skipsey

Doing repairs on a truck – welding is a valuable skill to have in the Outback.

Set in the Western MacDonnells, these incredible palm trees to be found only 50 kilometres south of Amburla thrive on the climate and desert soils. A true oasis.

Photo by Hans Boessem

My favourite reptile, the spectacular Perenty, Australia's largest lizard. This fellow is over a metre long, roaming proudly through the Aussie bush like the king he is.

Photo by Hans Boessem

Dad and me in the early morning, heading off to muster after camping out.
We are good mates.

Running brumbies into a portable yard at Amburla. Once broken in, brumbies can make
good stock horses – sure-footed and with plenty of stamina.

These amazing wildflowers are in abundance after winter rain in the desert.
This is in the Musgrave Ranges near Fregon, south of Alice Springs, where Rex and I built
camel yards for the aboriginal community there.

Photo by Hans Boessem

Major Mitchell cockatoos taking a drink of water out of a cattle trough, alert to any danger,
wearing their spectacular warpaint and headdress – they are real characters of the Outback.

Photo by Hans Boessem

Half a kilometre from Amburla Homestead, working stock with my mate
Brett Heaslip (left) in 1991 in the early days of promoting tourism.
The amazing Western Macs are in the background.

Photo by Steve Strike

A muster at Mistake Creek. In a muster we might move as many as 3000 cattle at one time –
notice the long trail of cattle continuing into the distance at the top of the photo.

The blue-tongue lizard – another of the Outback's funny little creatures, and one that even finds its way into the back yards of the cities. I wonder how it got its name?!

Photo by Hans Boessem

Chambers Pillar shows the contrasts in the country south of Alice, from desert sands to rocky outcrops. This was a unique landmark for pioneers travelling from Adelaide to Alice Springs, and of course part of many aboriginal myths.

Photo by Hans Boessem

Me breaking in a young horse – another essential skill of a stockman.

Photo by Bill Leimbach for Becker Entertainment

Trephina Gorge in the Eastern MacDonnell Ranges – another special spot to roll out
the swag and enjoy the simple things in life.

Photo by Hans Boessem

The honey ant – a delicacy of the Outback and a favourite of the Aborigines.

Photo by Hans Boessem

Me in my chopper – my answer to freedom. It's the only machine that has saved more lives than it's taken. A great tool on the land, saving precious time.

Me and my Uncle Scottie, a top mate and singing legend, trying on some new Outback Legend products.

Another dry season is evident as the south-easterly wind sends out ominous warnings.
Is there another drought around the corner? A dust storm on the edge of the Simpson Desert.
Photo by Hans Boessem

The Outback legend itself: the mighty wedge-tailed eagle surveying
the land below for its prey.
Photo by Hans Boessem

On the set of 'Outback Adventures', mustering horses in the Eastern MacDonnell Ranges, 80 kilometres east of Alice Springs.

Photo by Bill Leimbach for Becker Entertainment

At work on the 'Outback Adventure' series. I've had a bit of experience with these very intelligent creatures, capturing wild camels on our own properties and helping to set up special yards on local Aboriginal stations with the aim of selling the camels to the tourist industry.

In the Kimberley, doing some action-packed filming for 'Outback Adventures'.
I was about to jump the tidal waterfalls 200 metres ahead in saltwater crocodile and shark
territory. I ended up having to jump through eight times. Nothing like pure adrenaline!

Photo by Bill Leimbach for Becker Entertainment

Me with my friends' children from neighbouring properties filming *Outback Adventures for
Kids* produced on video through Polygram (Universal). I want kids to see our country as a
great big playground that they can get out into and enjoy, learn from and respect.

CHAPTER 15

THE ERADICATION YEARS

People on the land in Australia do it hard compared to a lot of our overseas competitors, who often receive subsidies from their respective governments. These subsidies are designed to compensate them for agriculture losses they've endured and to protect trade systems that often have nothing to do with fair competition but everything to do with unfairly controlling a market for whatever political agenda.

You tear your hair out sometimes in frustration at the things that happen overseas you have absolutely no control over, policies that can completely destroy your livelihood, your family and the work that perhaps three, four or five generations have put in to making something of themselves and the place they love.

So we modern pastoralists have got to be on top of all the challenges. And in recent decades there have been a few.

One issue that affects us all is the identification of sacred sites and how we can work with local Aborigines to steer clear of them. It's a partnership that allows everyone ready to bend their back to the task to make a future for themselves and all who come after them.

Now, there was a point a while back when everywhere that had a claim on it as a sacred site had supposedly been identified and listed (by the Sunset Clause date), and from then on anyone who was unsure about where they were about to run cattle, dig for gold, or go fishing could check that list and know whether they had a free run or had to start thinking again.

That list was locked off but, since then, when someone puts it about that they intend to open some country for cattle or dig under a mountain for diamonds, you can bet that bottom dollar nine times out of ten someone will pop up with a sacred site claim on it. A sacred site that all too often becomes bandied about by lawyers who set out to twist as much money as they can out of anyone wanting to get within cooee of that site. When work does start, that bottom dollar is buried under so many dollars spent getting to it, the pastoralist, miner or fishing company asks themselves why they bothered in the first place.

So more and more people turn to the city for income, dejected, disillusioned and knowing full well that the future of their children will be worse because of it.

Of course, this isn't always the case. Left to the locals, sensible and sensitive sacred site arrangements are often made that never feature on the front pages of city newspapers or in the lists of Supreme Court sittings, and work gets done with everybody sharing in the rewards. But all you need is someone spotting a chance to milk a system tilted towards dragging out what a handshake used to see sorted out in no short order, and it's years before the dust settles.

What we have to look towards is the future, making sure that nobody who wants to live and work out here will be denied that choice. Isn't that what real freedom is in a democracy? Choice to live how and where you want as long as that doesn't deny the person next to you the same thing? Well, for most of us out here, we'd choose the Outback every time, despite the challenges.

One other such challenge is disease, and the period I was working up at Mistake Creek was a busy and important time in the history of Australian pastoralism – the eradication years. A concentrated effort was put in over the last years of the eighties to wipe out brucellosis and tuberculosis from all the herds in the bush.

The diseases had taken hold of some of our stock because generations of cattle had been brought in from the wild, making careful stock management difficult. All stock had to be tested, including the wild buffaloes that were getting about all over the Top End, but cattle had picked up the infections from shared drinking and mixing together.

Tens of thousands of feral donkeys as well as wild horses (brumbies) were put down in the northern and Kimberley areas. They were pests that had built up in huge numbers, just like the camels that had gone feral since they'd been replaced by more modern modes of transport. The feral donkeys and horses were doing damage to the environment and eating out fodder. But this gives you an idea of how rich the Top End area is, that it's able to support such huge numbers of animals.

On the other hand, if left unchecked, those vast herds of feral animals, would have overrun the Territory, which translates into ruined watercourses, eroded landscapes, eaten-out

native plants and grasses and whole species of extinct indigenous animals unable to compete for food and water.

The priority of those days was cleaning up any disease in
Australian cattle herds. Being dependent on exporting our
cattle product, we had to eradicate any disease that countries
we exported to demanded. In reality, I've been told that some
of those countries still have T.B. in their stock today.

Although some of the scares were blown up a little – a lot,
as a matter of fact – by our competitors and crazy trade practices, no self-respecting Australian pastoralist wanted to be
breeding and selling anything but the best product they could.

There was nothing for it, because a health inspector's neg-
ative report is the final word when you're talking about meat
being fit for human consumption. The beef industry had to
clean out the diseases and restore the worldwide reputation of
Australian beef.

It proved to be an extended and often heart-breaking
process, but in the long run it left us where we are today, with
the cleanest stock on the face of the planet. The head count
of stock was hugely reduced, but the quality of our product
was raised to such a high standard that, allowing for the political bastardry that goes on in regard to access to foreign
markets, an Australian beef producer can honestly look you in
the eye and say there's no better or healthier meat being produced anywhere in the world. Lots of people, me included,
are worried about the use of drugs to produce quicker growth
rates in animals for human consumption, but it doesn't happen
in chemically free arid Australia!

The eradication had to be undertaken, of course, but unfortunately it wasn't the most reliable process the world's ever
seen. Stock were checked for disease by running them through

a race – a narrow-panelled corridor between large yards – and giving each of them a small injection in the caudal fold at the butt of the tail. This involved thousands of cattle, and it was very intensive and hands-on. It was a huge exercise in time and money.

Then, seventy-two hours later, you had to yard them all, then put them back through the race to check for reactions to the injection, which appeared as a lump on the inner caudal fold of the tail. Again the job involved one-by-one close inspection work.

Now, nobody begrudged putting in the work, because we all knew our futures as pastoralists with a competitive product were at stake. But I remember feeling at the time that it wasn't doing the stock much good. Cows and their calves were being separated, and the trauma of going twice through the race in a week, with all the unfamiliar noise, hurry and crowding, had an impact on every animal. People think that cows are dumb beasts and won't be affected by such treatment, but there's a mile of difference between animals treated with some sort of consideration and those shunted around like so much dead meat.

So the procedure was hard on the beasts and tough on everyone working them. When you did find a reactor to the initial injection, the veterinarian would put the animal down and then do a further test for disease. Just as often they'd find nothing – the reaction had been for some other reason.

Cattle that passed the tests had the plastic tags attached to their ears notched, so that anyone reading the tag could see how often a beast had been tested. In some cases they were tested twice a year.

In one instance, a cow had seven marks on her tag, which

showed she'd passed the test over several years. She'd had the injections in the tail and a clean bill of health when she was tested a day or two later. She went through, followed a little later by a twelve-month-old weaner that showed a reaction. They put some water paint on the weaner's head, then let it out into the yard.

The next day, they found the cow with the seven notches tagged with paint on her udder, so they knew she was the diseased weaner's mother. Now, bear in mind, she'd never shown up as diseased using the test that pastoralists had been routinely and back-breakingly applying to their stock for the previous years.

When the vet put her down and did an autopsy, he found she was riddled with T.B. That's where some of the heartbreak came in. Not only was the system killing large numbers of animals, but the test was sometimes inefficient so it seemed you might just as well have been doing nothing.

So the bottom line was that your calf crop was down, there were the effects on the stock of too much handling, and cattle from infected properties could only be sold to abattoirs for slaughter. So in some cases you were restricted to the one market, without having the option of interstate or store cattle sales.

I have to take my hat off to Dad because, like everyone in the eighties, on top of the tough eradication years he was having to meet the punitive interest rates that were around at the time, which were something like 23⅓ per cent compounding every month. Running costs never dropped during all that time: wages, fuel costs and everything else tied up with keeping a station productive were the same or getting higher, so in Dad's situation he had to make 28 per cent over all the outgoings to even start to smell a profit.

Others couldn't do it. Their start-out bottom lines were even tougher, or their herd was worse off, or their hearts just broke too badly to mend. But at the end of the long hard days they were gone, and the Territory was a lot poorer for losing some very good people.

As things have turned out, the eradication program succeeded. Our free-ranging cattle in arid Australia are top quality and they should be bringing top dollar on the world market.

Most pasturalists were given some assistance by the government for the hard times, such as compensation for animals eradicated and long-term, low-interest loans for infrastructure such as fences and yards. If there was any criticism it could have been the deadline that was set to have this campaign completed. Perhaps a five-year extension would have allowed for a lot more beasts to be captured.

The improved quality of the cattle should have been the very least to have come out of that tough time for Australia, and with the amount of money paid by pastoralists to the government in killing-fee levies for promoting this unique product, we should, in my view, be well ahead on the international stage for the healthiest beef. But the government still has a lot more work to do through strong marketing campaigns, both nationally and internationally.

Brucellosis and T.B. really took their toll on the Australian herd. But one of the worst diseases in cattle I've ever seen in my life is botulism. It's transferred from the carcasses of dead animals. Botulism turns up in the newspapers every now and then because it's one of the most feared bacteria. I've heard that the equivalent of a cup full of botulism bacteria, put into the world's water supply, could wipe out every human being on earth. And, wouldn't you know it, the stuff is stored in laboratories all over the planet, just in case World War III breaks out and someone reckons the extinction of mankind is a fair way to achieve national pride, ethnic cleansing or whatever other mad idea seems to get hold of people during wartime.

In livestock, it's most often an accident of nature. I'd never seen the disease before till one day when I was working at Mistake Creek with Dad, Dad's old mate Smacka, a group of Top End Aboriginal stockmen who'd worked with us for some time and my old friend Colin from Waite River days. We were shifting 1500 head of cattle and had walked them about 25 kilometres when we came upon a waterhole. They were thirsty, so we let them have a drink and a bit of a breather, and then moved them on to meet up with another mob of about 500 cattle in the next paddock.

But when we got up to the fence line, I'd never seen anything like it. There were about 50 cattle in sight, some of them scattered about lying on the ground, kicking their legs, some of them trying to stand. It was cruel, like something out of a nightmare. There was one mob going through hell and another lot separated by nothing more than a fence still looking healthy and well-looked after. To add to the weirdness, the sick cattle that weren't flat on the ground were running around crazily, some of them backwards, doing cartwheels. You wouldn't believe it without seeing it, and maybe if you didn't know the poor animals were in such a bad way, it might have looked like some sort of tightly worked-out circus routine to amuse paying customers. But it wasn't the tiniest bit funny.

Dad figured it out first. He'd never seen the effects of botulism, either, but he'd heard over the bush telegraph about the signs to look for. We worked out that they might have had a drink from that waterhole we'd just used, and perhaps there'd been a carcass in it from a previous flood, we couldn't know for sure, that had poisoned the water.

It was one of the saddest thing I'd ever seen. The animals were really suffering from the maddening effects of the disease, and there was nothing we could do about it.

Dad was hurt, not only because he was watching weeks of hard work come to nothing, but because he loved his stock and prided himself on being on top of most of the hard challenges the Territory can throw at a cattleman. Nothing can prepare you or your animals for sheer bad luck or Nature's occasional dirty tricks, but that doesn't make a proud man feel any better when he's confronted with a scene like this one.

There was nothing at all we could do, of course, but having to walk through this mob with rifles to put the animals out of their misery didn't add anything but more sadness to the day.

And then we weren't sure whether we were right about that waterhole and whether our mob had been affected, too.

As it turned out, the mob we had with us didn't pick up the botulism, so the poor creatures on the far side of the fence must've got it from another water supply, or by some other way. It was a tough few days, though, watching for the first sign of trouble.

Sometimes out here it seems that if the weather or the distances or the interest rates don't get you, something else will. Disease is just another challenge you take on, and it can be a tough, heart-breaking battle. But if you want the best product, you've got to beat it, and keep beating it. And during that time working up at Mistake Creek the quality of our stock just got better and better. So it was a battle well worth fighting.

CHAPTER 16

GETTING AROUND THE OUTBACK – THE QUICK WAY

You don't see Dad angry very often, but after we found those poor animals infected with botulism he was upset. And at that stage we still didn't know whether the cattle we were moving had been infected.

There was nothing we could do but put them down. So with the dead cattle behind us and the sun setting before us we kept going, because the cattle we were driving needed to be in the yards before dark or we'd have a hell of a night ahead keeping them together. I kept out of Dad's way up ahead, riding the left wing, with a couple of stockman out front with Colin leading the way. Smacka was off to another side with his blue-heeler, one of the smartest dogs I've ever seen working, taking part of the wing all by herself a good 200 metres from us.

But, smooth as things were going considering, Dad was still

167

in a sad mood, and both Smacka and I got the sharp edge of his tongue as the afternoon crawled into night. Smacka and I just gave each other a look at one stage, shrugged as if to say, 'Let's just keep out of his way and get the job done', and got on with it. But while the sky was as clear as purest crystal, there were storm clouds thick and rumbling on my Dad's face.

Unfortunately, the storm was about to break. We did get the cattle to the yards, a little late, but safe for the night. And we did get the saddles off the horses, giving our mounts a good rub down with the horse blankets to dry the sweat off them where it builds up under the saddles. You do that because that's where the horse's kidneys are, and a chill setting in there brings a horse down with a cold as quickly as you or me. So, we'd had enough after a long, hard, bitter day. All of us were look-ing forward to a meal, some tea and some sleep.

The one thing the last bloke through the gate hadn't done was shut it. Well, you'd have thought those horses would've had enough for the day, too, but no, show a horse an open gate and he'll be through it if the wide blue yonder and a bigger paddock of grass lies beyond it. Especially with the moon lighting up the impenetrable black night of Outback Australia.

The horses were gone in a flurry of hooves, dust and curses from my old man. Dad fingered me, saying it was my fault because it had been my responsibility to see the job was done. He was right in my face and rightly so as it was my responsi-bility. Without a thought and with a length of hay twine the only thing in my hands, I ran over to one of the few horses still there, slipped the twine over its head, looping it around its nose as a makeshift neck rein, leapt on to her bare back, swung her head around and kicked her after her mates.

The faint moonlight, small blessing, gave me some idea of

my way but it was a mad ride. I had only minimal control over the mount, the main mob had a Melbourne Cup field lead on me and I didn't know what was ahead of me, whether there were ditches, rocks or fallen trees that my horse and I might power into with no warning. But I knew they were running towards a corner in the fence line, and if I stayed behind them I'd almost certainly panic the mob into the fence, doing damage to them.

I gave my horse her head and cut through some scrub, trusting in fate and other kindnesses I've probably had more advantage of than a man deserves. The horse was giving me her all, so much so that I could only get her to turn right by pulling on that loose rein as I reached forward to cup her left eye with my hand. She got the idea from this temporary blinkering and the tugs of the hay twine rein, but I was still operating on a wing and a prayer. Luckily for me, it paid off.

My mount and I jumped through the scrub right in front of the escapee mob, most of them pretty much run in by now, anyway, after the race for open country on top of a hard day's work. I pulled them up, told them to get themselves home, and they did. They turned around and followed the fence line all the way back to the yards.

Horses are very intelligent animals. They say a dog is a man's best friend, and watching Smacka's great little bluey working cattle all afternoon, I wouldn't have had a counter argument to that point of view. But there's a special bond between horses and humans that is just as remarkable. When you really bond with a horse it's the sort of understanding and unspoken minute-to-minute exchange that can't be put into words. Which is probably why a horse would understand better what I'm trying to say here than you might!

I guided the mob back into the yard, cut the makeshift rein off my own horse with my pocket knife, walked out of the yard, made sure the gate was securely shut behind me, and turned around into the full explosion of a slow-brewing thunderstorm.

Dad was mad, even more so now after seeing me do what he told me was the craziest thing he'd ever seen me do, and lord knows, he'd seen me do a few. On he went: where must my brains be riding out into the dark like that, and did I think about the horse, or me, or him or what he'd have had to tell Mum when they brought me in in a neck brace or worse?

I waited him out: I could see his point, but I could also see my own. Then I told him that the horses were back where he'd wanted them first thing tomorrow, and that whatever had gone wrong today we'd best put behind us, because tomorrow didn't look any lighter a work load, from where I was standing, so we should leave it at that.

We did. And that's another reason why we're good mates today: he let me have my own say and to be strong in my belief, to stand up and be counted. For that I've always respected him and I've only admiration for him.

It can be hard to work with your old man at times, but work together and communicate, and it can be fun. If you haven't got family what have you got?

So I walked past Smacka and went off to lay out my swag. Smacka winked at me, I reckon, though I might have been seeing things, because he's always had a funny way with his right eye when he's around Dad and me.

A few days later, when we realised the cattle hadn't been infected by the botulism, tension in the camp lessened. I was just happy to be out there doing what I liked best with blokes who knew what they were about – except for the occasional gate, that is. Which once more brought back to me the old equation of responsibility and danger that another gate had introduced me to a decade or so before.

❖　❖　❖

Much as I love saddling a good horse and riding out at a pace nature might have intended, I'm also pretty addicted to the speed and excitement that only a motor bike can give you.

When you're riding around central Australia off the beaten track, which is a matter of seconds from where you started, you can see pretty clearly any obstacles ahead. There's no really long grass to hide holes or boulders or fallen logs. It's not as smooth as silk, but watch out for gilgais, creeks, thick mulga patches and the odd anthill and you can usually make your own safe path.

But up in the Top End, which can be really lush in a good season, ant beds and the long, black, spear grass sit up like a wide carpet over the landscape, and you've got no idea what's below. The simple answer to that, of course, is easy as she goes, but if you did that every minute of the day, you'd get nothing done.

Once, we were waiting on the plant horses to get the muster cracking, so I moved them quickly back through the first paddock. Approaching the yards, a couple of them turned around and tried to duck back. When that lead's given you can lose the whole mob, especially if you're running brumbies and the dominant mare's the one making the break. You see, much as the world might think it's the big old stallion that rules a bunch of horses, the fact is, horses as a mob follow a dominant mare, the female who has the edge on the other mares as far as keeping the group manageable. The stallion is so busy making sure no other stallion knocks him off the reproductive perch, so to speak, the day-to-day job of keeping the family in line falls to Big Mama.

Anyway, I was on a trail bike with 98 per cent of the horses doing what I wanted, while a couple of horses made a break for it. I spun around after them, and luckily they were just a couple of young fillies that the rest of the mob didn't take a lead from, so it was quick work wheeling them back into the tail end of the main mob going into the yards. But, finishing off the process, I rode straight into a ditch masked over by that long grass. I hit a log, I mean a *big* log, a metre wide.

It was enough to stop the bike dead. But not me. I will always remember it in slow motion, just as if I was in an animated movie, sliding forward, right up over the petrol tank, catching the petrol cap with, ah, some unprotected parts. Then I kept going, my legs up around the handle bars, my head dipping forward to end up pretty much level with the front wheel. The sound of the collision sank in, as the engine screamed then shut off as if I'd done this to it on purpose. My eyes were locked on the black knobby tyre right under my nose, the grass all around closing in like it was trying to cover over the scene of the crime, and that bloody great log just lying there with a smug look about it, like, 'Shit happens!'

But I was still moving, and floating around in my head was a thought along the lines of 'If only I'd gone left!' before I completed that arc right over the handle bars, crumpled up against the log, and rolled away to the left.

Lucky for me, this was all going on close enough for some

other blokes who'd been waiting on the horses to drive a four-wheel-drive ute up pretty quickly. I was in pain, and I've never been able to look at a petrol cap since without my eyes watering.

I managed to get up, dizzy and staggering, and found my way to sit on the back tailgate of the four-wheel-drive to get me back to the homestead!

Simone had some Radox she used to put in the bath to relieve aches and pains. She promised me that a good Radox bath would wave the magic wand over every painful portion of me, which was about every square inch and 2 inches deep with it. So she ran the bath, and I peeled the jeans off, gingerly all the way, because those unprotected parts of my anatomy had swelled up with the rough treatment from the bike. For all the pain that I was feeling as I slipped into the bath, I had to ask Simone: 'This Radox stuff. It'll take away the pain, right, but can it leave the swelling?'

CHAPTER 17

....

MAKING PLANS AROUND
THE CAMPFIRE

I was twenty years old, had a few experiences under my belt
and had learnt a few skills as well. Which was lucky, because
one Sunday when I was at Amburla I got an emergency call
from my good friend, Brett Heaslip, on Bond Springs Station.
Brett and I grew up together on neighbouring properties and
we always had a lot in common. Brett's of similar height and
build to me, and the girls like his blue eyes and good looks.

On this particular Sunday he needed me to do some
welding work on a bulldozer with a broken blade. I drove out
and spent the next five hours getting the machine back into
shape.

The property we were on had been working for a hundred
years or more, and it still had a couple of old-style wells on it,
basically holes in the ground with a wooden framework at
ground level for access and maintenance. I'd just finished the

welding when one of the girls ran over. She was upset because a young steer had fallen into one of the old wells. The steer was 5 metres down and just short of drowning.

Brett and I raced over and, sure enough, the steer was putting up a struggle down there to stay above water. But the effort was telling, and I could see that in another minute or two the beast would be a goner. Another worker who was there told me to stay clear of the old wood frame, as it was likely to give way under me. Well, seeing that poor animal in trouble was more important so, while Brett ran off to get a vehicle, I jumped down into the water with the steer.

I'm not too sure if the beast had the first idea why it was suddenly getting so crowded down there. But I wedged myself in one corner of the well, bracing my feet against the sides, grabbed the steer's horns and it seemed to understand I was there to help. I could keep its head above water because the full weight of the two-year-old steer was largely buoyed up by the water. The beast stopped kicking and was able to conserve its strength as I held its mouth clear for easier breathing. But we didn't have much room to go anywhere, as small pieces of bark and dirt showered us from above!

Brett turned up a few minutes later with a four-wheel-drive and a good length of rope. He tied one end off on the vehicle's bullbar, and hurled the other down to me. I looped the rope around the steer's horns and then Brett began to slowly reverse away from the edge. Holding on to the rope, the steer and I rose out of the water and up towards the opening above, swinging through space in an awkward embrace that no self-respecting circus aerialist would be caught doing.

The steer wasn't very happy about this, but the rope held around his horns, and with one of the jillaroos signalling Brett at the wheel of the four-wheel-drive, we were both dragged easy as she goes to the lip of the well. I clambered out ahead of the steer and then the animal slid up over the edge and on to firm land.

It just lay there for a minute or two, getting its breath back, and then clambered up onto its feet with our help. It shook the water off, gave Brett and me a look like, 'Thanks, if I can ever do the same for you . . .', and wandered away to join the rest of the mob.

That day stands out as one of the first times that Brett and I, 'the team of two', worked so well together. We've shared good times since, and have got in and out of our fair share of scrapes to become really close mates, with a lot of our friendship based on trust and confidence in each other.

Brett and I maintained a sort of working friendship: I'd help him out with the machinery on his property, and we'd work stock together. Along the way I became close to his family, too. But as we worked alongside each other we discovered that we also shared dreams that I hadn't really dealt with since I was fifteen when I had gone to Dad with the idea of going to acting school.

I'm not saying Dad hoped that the apprenticeship and what flowed on from it would keep me so busy that any thoughts about following the artistic bent in my personality would evaporate, but that's almost what had happened. I was flat out just doing what needed to be done on the family properties, and the idea of leaving Mum and Dad and my sisters in the lurch while I went off to try to become a TV or film star just didn't hold water against the next day's full roster.

But the thing is, busy as you are mustering or working on the innards of some huge machine, dreams don't just disappear.

The dreams I had were real ambitions, concrete intentions, not just fanciful wishes to avoid the hard yakka of Outback life. I knew that I had a voice of my own, and ideas to go with it, ideas that I hoped were at least the equal of anything I was seeing on television screens or at the cinema. So over the long miles of dust and sweat and cows, camels and horses, I was putting together the stories I wanted to tell and exactly how I would tell them, the pictures flickering in my imagination, even if I was a long way yet from working out exactly how to get them flickering on a silver screen for the whole world to share.

In Brett I discovered a real partner in these enthusiasms, a bloke who not only knew what I wanted to do was possible, but that it was worthwhile! You see, I was getting upset that Australia was so quickly becoming an urbanised country, and that we were losing sight of our own culture and the legacy of our pioneering ancestors. Everything I saw on TV when I got the chance – which wasn't often – seemed to be so Americanised. Hey, America is a great country and Americans are good people, but we're Australian and Australia is the wild west of the world – it's one of the last frontiers.

So I figured it was an important job, if not for my own sake then for our kids growing up, whatever race and whatever colour, to bring the Australian way of living that survives in the Outback to the world, to record it and help it to prosper. It could be done without compromising the lives we were living already. It was just a question of laying out a plan, working it step by step, and not getting ahead of ourselves – exactly the same procedure required to fix a broken machine, move a mob of animals a thousand kilometres, fly a helicopter, keep a working cattle station productive, or anything else we'd learnt living out here. But with the extra magic ingredient of creativity that Brett and I both knew we had to make entertainment, to tell stories and to entertain an audience.

Well, that's what we figured around many a campfire or side by side at a few bars or across a table or two, as we nutted out script ideas for feature movies. Anything was possible, we reckoned – still do – but for all that excitement and certainty, there was still the day's work to be done. So, thinking way into the future, planning what it would take to earn ourselves enough down time to really throw ourselves into developing some of our TV and film ideas, we'd jump into the next saddle, on to the next trail bike, behind the steering wheel of another machine or the joystick of an aeroplane or chopper and get on with the job at hand.

Part of the jobs at hand allowed me to share another pursuit that Brett and I both loved, which was flying. Brett also had a little Cessna 182 (a four-seater), and every now and then we'd fly over to the other's property and then on around the western MacDonnell Ranges. It was magic up there, flying through gorges, along the waterways, just soaking up the beauty of the area from above, from that bird's eye view we just as often shared with wedge-tailed eagles. I think that some of those fellas saw us as a bit of competition when it came to showing our skills off in the wide open airspace. I'd be flying with a wedgie alongside, and it would mirror my every move. I'd tilt my wings left, and it would follow, tit for tat. But, of course, the eagle always won out in the end because he could fly and land anywhere he chose, and just lift up into the sky on a whim. We, on the other hand, always had to find a safe place to land or we'd need to return to the homestead for fuel.

While we were up there Brett and I would practise precision flying, pretending we were having dog fights like the Red Baron and Biggles, and just putting the little machines through their paces, all of which helped tighten up our flying skills for musters.

But when we were on the ground, Brett and I put our heads together on ideas for a film we had, an Outback adventure which would show the place and the people living in it the way it really was. Because we felt that country people, in general, but Outback folk in particular, are all too often portrayed in locally made films as either colourful loud-mouthed lunatics or hayseeds without two brain cells to rub together. When in fact, head for head, mile for mile, country Australia's produced as many successful men and women in every pursuit of life you'd like to pick – artistic, scientific, business, sport, politics and entertainment – as the nation's cities. And those who choose to stay out back and work the land that still carries a large part of Australia's fortune and future are as up to date and clued-in in their chosen careers as anyone working in a skyscraper.

We're all Australians, all contributing to the story that every day makes this country a little richer, a little more developed in the only place that really counts, the heart and soul of its people. Pick up a pen, pick up a shovel, drive a roadtrain or a suburban bus, walk ten minutes to work across town or ride a horse three hours before dawn, lay out a paddock or a city block square, or clean offices way past midnight: we're all at the same task – getting by and putting something away for the next generation.

People work, people play, and somewhere in there the storytellers draw out the lessons and the insights, the joy and the despair, and weave it back into everyday lives, in books, painting, music and my special love, moving pictures.

So all the way Brett and I were taking raw materials and buffing them into stories that we felt would have something to say to Australians as well as something about Australia and its people to the rest of the world. We'd get together and yarn ideas into black and white on paper, then tear up that paper and start again with better ideas and more certain belief in our tale that needed telling.

Livings had to be made, daily bread earned, and I still had a hard lesson or three to learn along the way, especially about how the best-laid plans can go down the chute on you as easily as a curious steer falling down a well, and without always having as happy an ending.

CHAPTER 18

DREAMS IN NORTHERN AUSTRALIA

I guess I was a man with a mission. While I was hatching plans for films and TV shows, I also got to thinking about what I felt was a sadly under-developed resource. My family had a connection with Darwin and the coast up there. Darwin is the capital of the Northern Territory, Australia's northern-most city and very much the 'gateway' to our South-East Asian neighbours in Indonesia, the Philippines and Malaysia. The town was virtually wiped flat by Cyclone Tracy in 1974, and when it was rebuilt every effort was made to not only make it cyclone proof but to ensure it was well planned to make the most of it assets.

As a young bloke, along with others, I felt the town in the late eighties was crying out for an improvement to its harbour that would make it the gateway to the whole country and turn Darwin into the biggest and most important port in Australia.

If ships loaded and off-loaded here, with locally owned rail transport feeding them and delivering away from Darwin, the whole country could save millions of dollars spent paying (mostly) foreign-owned ships to travel the two or three thousand extra kilometres around the coast to Melbourne and Sydney.

Darwin is a picture, a beautiful place to live with such a melting pot of people living there some reckon it's a model for the whole country's future. Be that as it may, few other places in Australia are as well-placed (cyclones excepted) to foster a lifestyle that's unhurried, welcoming, supportive, modern and sophisticated, but not exclusive, all in one.

There have been plans for a rail line between Alice and Darwin since the days of Burke and Wills in the 1860s, probably. Where men, horses and camels eventually went, the rail men couldn't have been far behind. Except for the problems of distance and money.

And one or two other considerations, of course. I wouldn't want to point my finger too hard, but the long-time interests of established money in the bigger east-coast cities of Sydney, Melbourne and Brisbane have seen any sensible plans to develop Darwin fiercely nipped in the bud. Halfway down the stalk!

The dream of a cross-country line still lives, with plans on the drawing board to properly link Alice Springs and Darwin by rail. Not before time, either. But even if the rail link had been there in the late eighties, there was still the opportunity to improve Darwin's harbour.

While doing my trade with McMahons I'd met a fella called Dick, a dozer operator. Along with dozing he also had twenty years' experience working large dredges, most of it around Saudi Arabia and Cuba.

We'd got to talking one night, and we worked out that if we could get our hands on a dredge, no matter what its condition, I could help get it up and running again. He'd drive the machine, and we could reclaim a lot of land in Darwin Harbour, where much of the coastline is so shallow that access needs to be dredged out for the larger vessels. Once we had the business on a good footing and with a couple of extra blokes on the payroll, we'd not only be making a good go of it for ourselves, we could contribute to the plans afoot to turn Darwin into just the sort of major harbour it could have been for years.

We signed a deal, made ourselves a partnership with a company and were ready to go. I put most of my savings into the fledgling company, including setting the office up in a local house with all the necessary equipment, like faxes and computers, as well as financing a car for Dick to get around in.

We were looking great guns, and the first part of the job actually saw our company doing the government a good turn. Before you did any dredging you had to send down divers to bring up core samples of what was on the bottom. The bottom of Darwin's harbour, unlike Sydney's, which I understand is littered with tricky business arrangements, is actually home to all sorts of odds and ends left over from the Second World War. The divers had to ascertain whether there were any unexploded bombs on the site because, oddly enough, local dredge drivers have a little hang-up about being blown sky high on the job. So anyone doing a survey of the bottom of the harbour is saving the authorities the job, and if they find something and it is safely removed, they're doing the whole community a favour at the same time.

I was working closely with a government department as

we went along, but it was in the very early days of the authorities putting themselves and their budgets wholeheartedly into
improving Darwin Harbour. There were ordinances to be
passed, bills to be signed, bureaucracies to be staffed – the
whole kit and caboodle. All of which boiled down to not a
lot of money around to get things done, which meant most of
the tabs were being ticked off with the help of Dick and me.

Every businessman has to watch money go out before it
starts to flow back in, so while I wasn't actually leaping for joy
over the monthly figures, the chats I was having with people
in government had me fairly confident that, in the long run,
I'd have official assistance to see the project through.

All the time, while Dick stayed up in Darwin running the
company, I'd be down at Mistake Creek, feeding back enough
cash to keep things ticking over. This went on for about a year
and a half, without things looking much better than when we'd
started out. Dick approached me about leasing the station's
dozer so he could pick up a bit of extra work dozer driving
on some of the new properties around Darwin and Katherine
that needed roads and dams built.

I asked Dad about it and worked out an hourly rate that
he okayed, probably because he figured that if Dick was
earning something off his own back I might see a little less
pressure on my bank account.

I delivered the dozer on the back of a truck and left it with
Dick before making the drive south to Amburla to finish off
the mustering season. Dad was staying on at Mistake Creek.

Christmas came up quickly. It was hot and dry, too hot to
move cattle around much. I figured, since I had the truck and
some enforced time on my hands, I'd take up a job offer that

the station received to cart wheat from Esperance, on the south coast of Western Australia.

If you look at a map you'd probably reckon I was mad. Esperance is as far from Darwin as Adelaide and on roads about three times less easy to travel. It was basically driving from the top of the country to the bottom for a short-term job. But for those of us living in the Outback, distance just *is* – you don't think about it like someone who travels an hour to work and back in the city every day and feels whacked out by the end of the trip.

Besides, the truck was on hand, the bank account was out of control and the job was going. Decision made.

I leased the truck from the family station, took up as much work as I could in Western Australia, and with a school mate called Craig along for the ride and the job in his own truck, I would maybe clear a thousand dollars a week or more that could go into keeping the dredging company afloat. The dredging contracts that were in the offing were close enough to sniff, both Dick and I were convinced, so this period of outside work by both of us would tide the company over and service the growing debts to the banks in one hit.

Another friend, Normie, had signed on, too, so we all headed out from Alice Springs pretty much like we were going on a boys' own adventure. I had two trailers behind the White Road Boss, and Craig's truck up on the trailer, as he was to travel across in his ute a couple of days later. All our tools and tyres and any other maintenance gear was on the back of the second trailer, everything tied down and secure for the long journey ahead. Fleetwood Mac was in the cassette player.

We were about an hour south of Alice, with night coming on, when I decided to pull over and check the load. I guided the truck over the top of a hill and down. We were doing about 70 kilometres an hour when, fair out of nowhere, four cattle ran straight in front of us. I didn't have time to hit the brakes or anything before we were on them, with all the momentum of the two laden trailers behind the main rig pushing us along.

A couple of beasts went straight under the truck and the first damage they caused was to bend the tie rod ends, which are the steering arms. The result was the two front wheels of my truck turned in facing each other, leaving me with no steering whatsoever, exactly at the point where the road veered away to the left, with a 4-metre drop straight ahead. The truck just powered straight on, and I figured this was goodnight for us. I'd probably be waking up in hospital if I was lucky. Really lucky.

The truck jack-knifed as it went off the edge, with the first trailer and the truck on it now visible from my window, all of us moving in this screeching mess of everything gone wrong, my mind processing what I was seeing, but just saying over and over again like a machine locked on replay: 'Wrong wrong wrong.' Well, something went right, although it's all relative in the way these things go. The A-frame to the last trailer had snapped off when it hit the bitumen, so that load had gone off in another direction where it couldn't do us any harm. Out of sight, out of mind. And even though a sudden jolt broke the chains and catapulted the truck out of the trailer still linked to us, that jolt and our momentum was enough to see it fly straight over the cabin of my vehicle. It collected some trees, came to earth with a crash I can still hear if I want to (but I don't) and came to a halt.

Then our vehicle caught the trees and pulled up hard, with the engine still vibrating and dust we'd thrown up all over us.

There was so much dust in the cabin, I couldn't even see Normie in there with me. I didn't know what was next. I sat there for maybe a minute waiting for the sky to fall in, or whatever next disaster fate had in store for us. But nothing happened.

I had blood running down over my face because I'd bounced up and hit the square metal box of the CB radio with the top of my head, and it had split the skin there. I called out to Normie to see if he was all right, but he'd already jumped out of the passenger side, and he yelled back he was okay. I climbed out of the truck and all I could see was wreckage. The truck that had flown over us was completely ruined; the one I'd been driving was halfway to the wrecker's yard.

After all the things that hadn't gone through my head, like trucks, tools or tyres, what was racketing around inside my skull were the craziest thoughts: I seemed to be the Territory's number one living target for accidents with rolled cars, bent bikes and now I had a busted-up roadtrain on my résumé. What I should have been thinking about, I suppose, was how all my well-laid plans for getting the dredging company solvent were now so much twisted metal and scattered good intentions.

But sitting on the edge of the highway in the dark, with my shirt wrapped around my head to staunch the flow of blood, I soon had other thoughts to occupy my mind. Thoughts about people, and the funny way they can treat you from one look and a tickle of the old preconception bone. Normie waved down a car, and they pulled up alongside me with a shirt on my head that was just about soaked through by now. I must have looked like I needed help four ways from Sunday, really pathetic, you couldn't imagine anyone's heart wouldn't go out to me, the innocent victim of a dreadful accident.

Bull. The driver hit the accelerator after one good look at me and the car roared off in fumes and gravel that spat back all over us. We couldn't believe it. I mean, okay, they couldn't see the truck way off the road in the dark, so my mate and I could've been lunatics about to do mayhem, but . . .

Five minutes later a four-wheel-drive came to the rescue and gave the two of us a lift into town where I spent a couple of days in hospital.

Mum and Dad were really relieved that I'd survived yet another close shave, but I could see Dad knew I was really flattened by the whole thing. He'd claim insurance on the truck but my plans to get the dredging company back in the black by the trip to Esperance were down the gurgler. I was sitting in hospital looking like an elephant had tap-danced all over my skull, and if the word 'bleak' needed spelling I could have come up with fifteen variations on it tagged on to that other word – 'future'.

CHAPTER 19

....

R.I.P. M.L.P.

As things panned out, though, the accident was a turning point in my life. In an effort to gee me up and give me a new focus, Dad told me about a sale of Brahman cattle that was starting up the next week. Called the Celebrity Classic, it was going off in Rockhampton, in Queensland. The best of the Brahman cattle in Australia would be there.

'You've always liked Brahman cattle,' Dad said, remembering that I'd been fascinated by the beasts ever since my Uncle Max got some on to his property. They're magnificent animals: with their big, noble heads and that great hump on the back of their necks they all look like individuals. (Laugh if you like, but when I look out over a mob of our Brahmans, I can pick some of them out by name for you.)

What I knew about them then was the breed we called Brahmans were originally from India, but had gone through some breeding changes in the United States. Changes that made them bigger and even more resilient in tough conditions. They were hardy animals and tick resistant, which is a really big issue in our part of the world, where blood-poisoning ticks can weaken a mob in short shrift. I also knew that Brahman cows were good mothers. They have a really small calf so the births are generally easy, and they bond closely with their offspring. A fluent animal, they can walk out a lot further than any other British or European breeds, so in the big paddocks which are the defining reality of Outback stations with drought conditions thrown in three times out of five, they were the ideal beast for breeding here.

Dad had heard me going on about Brahmans often enough, and didn't take much convincing himself. He knew he could sell them to Asia and give us a second market. Dad goes with the times.

This Rockhampton sale sounded like the good oil, and with the disappointment of my partnership with Dick floundering, topped off by thousands of dollars worth of damaged trucks and trailers on the road outside of Alice, Dad knew right away I needed to get myself enthused about something for the quickest route back onto my feet.

Dad had already done enough homework around Mistake Creek and the adjoining Top End properties to recognise that more good bulls were needed up there to restore the quality of the herds, especially following the extreme reduction of cattle numbers due to the eradication program.

'If you want to do it,' he said, 'the market for bulls is there sure enough. You could start that stud property you've always talked about.' He knew he was talking to the converted, of course, and from that moment, just about all I could think

of was getting out of hospital, up to Rockhampton and checking what was on offer.

A day or two later Dad and I had flown into Rocky and
bought ourselves some stock. Once they were back on home
ground, I started breeding some good strong lines of animal
from our core beasts. Along the way I had to pick up some
qualifications and skills in artificial impregnation techniques
and pregnancy testing so that we could keep an organised and
scientific eye on building up our new herd. I never quite saw
myself in a white lab coat with a test tube in one hand and a
thermometer in the other, but the whole process of building
up and improving our stock was further proof that to survive
and prosper out here you need to be Professor Jack-of-all-
sciences while you're about it.

We must have been doing something right because our
animals were pretty quickly winning prizes and championship
certificates at agricultural shows. I was really proud one year
when Dad let me pick out the animals for the carcass competition at Alice Springs. There were four classes in the comp:
the Baby Teeth, the Two Year Old, the Three Year Old and
the Japanese Steer, which are destined for the feed-lots for
priming for the Japanese market. We won in all four classes,
which proved we'd established excellent bloodlines, and that
helped us kick-start the sale of some of our bulls around the
region.

The stud business was very expensive to set up for the
station but it was going well. I was in there hands-on all the
way, and the prizes and sales that came along made me feel
particularly proud. But that was nothing compared to the pride
I'd feel just standing in the same yard at home with a beast I'd
helped create by making breeding decisions a generation or

two back, before it came into the world and became not only a champion but living proof of what we'd set out to do to improve and expand the viability of the breed as a whole.

Maybe none of this would have come to be except that I rolled a roadtrain on the road out of Alice. So, out of one of the worst moments of my life till then came some of the best experiences I've ever had. In saying that, I hope you don't have to crash a truck to change the track of your life. There have to be easier ways!

❖   ❖   ❖

Life's a fragile thing anywhere on earth, and holding on to it can sometimes seem more luck than good management. Because, just like those cows came out in front of the roadtrain, there's no telling when the simplest thing you've done a hundred times before can go wrong.

Not long after we had the first Brahmans from Rockhampton bedded down in their new home at Amburla I was showing an English backpacker the sights of nearby Standley Chasm. She was like many of the travellers who come through our part of the world, passing by, picking up a little work on the way and then moving on. She'd done some mustering with us and picked up some stationhand skills around the home block, but now she was heading for northern parts.

I drove her into the chasm on the way into Alice, where she'd connect with the main road, and we were looking over the truly magnificent scenery of the place. The chasm itself is a slit in the MacDonnell Ranges, 60 or 70 metres high with rusty orange quartzite walls. There are points where the chasm is no more than 5 metres wide, so it would stand in as a perfect ambush point in a Hollywood Western.

Generally, though, there's nothing blood-red here but the last of the sunset splashing over the chasm walls, which is what gets the tourists in and occasionally has the place as chock-a-block as Central Station in Sydney come rush hour. There are other attractions here, too, because the chasm's at one end of a wet gully overflowing with ferns and the local MacDonnell Ranges cycads.

It's one of those places, up there with Uluru and Katatjuta (The Olgas), that you can't leave the Centre without seeing. I figured a little local knowledge on my part would give this lady another layer of insight into what she was looking at for almost certainly the last time in her life, before she returned to England and her old life.

We were standing just short of the imposing gap in the mountain range, which always looks to me like it's about to slam shut with some great mountainous voice laughing out, 'Gotcha!' Just as we were about to leave, a ranger rode up on a small four-wheel motor bike.

He handed me a hessian bag as he clambered off his vehicle. 'Hang on to this for a tick, mate,' he said. I took the sack, but didn't get a clean enough hold on it, because a snake came leaping out of the thing and coiled itself around my arm, ending up with its head raised, looking me fair in the eye.

I was taken aback, but quickly enough recognised that at least it was only a python, not a poisonous king brown or worse.

The English girl had leapt away and was now peering over my shoulder. Looking at me face to face with the snake, she said, 'That snake's going to bite you Troy.'

'Ah, I'm a boy from the bush,' I said. 'He won't bite me. He's an old mate.'

Yeah, well so much for mate. This one had been a bush snake all his life, and he figured he'd get the jump on anyone he liked.

Wham! The snake's head darted at my forearm, its fangs going straight into the flesh. And then again, two bites into me. Now, I knew the snake was a python, but you can never be entirely sure you haven't picked up a lookalike, or some sort of cross-breed. So, with blood streaming down my arm, I stood there looking at the ranger, with an expression on my face that said, 'How long have I got, Doc?'

I let the snake go in the bushes as the ranger requested, and turned to a rather pale-faced English girl, who was in shock by now.

'Are you okay?' she said.

'I'll be fine,' I said, then heard a voice inside me say, 'Where do you think you get off trying to be cool?' I was sure it was only a matter of time before I'd start to get dizzy spells!

So it was not much of a day all round for anyone but the angry python who was back in his territory.

I still wasn't a hundred per cent sure that it was only a python, but I felt okay after I'd cleaned up the blood and soaked the four holes in my arm with Dettol.

We finished the trip into town and I waved my friend goodbye, half expecting all the time to keel over. But it didn't happen, so I came through with nothing but a tender arm and another lesson from Outback life – when the hessian bags are being handed around, pass.

The big problems still remained, however. A dredging company not doing anywhere near enough dredging, a bank manager making a lot of phone calls and a grand idea that was way ahead of its time about to go belly up because a whole lot of promises had turned into hessian bags – empty except for the totally unlooked-for coming at you with fangs bared.

Dick got together with another bloke up in Darwin and started leasing brand new road-working equipment, which the company would then lease on to the big projects that were coming up. The pressure was getting to Dick, as it was getting to me, and the projects were so far off all we had was brand spanking new machinery sitting idle and costing the company a fortune – a fortune we didn't have.

It turns out the bloke Dick was taking advice from was basically taking money from us, with Dick and me none the wiser as the fellow spun huge business plans to him.

The wash-up of it all was that there was nothing left in the kitty to meet any of the costs the company had signed up for. Dick declared bankrupt and went back home to New Zealand. But I had to live and work here in the Territory with people I could reasonably expect to have many more dealings with in the future. There was no way that at twenty-one years of age I was going to declare bankruptcy. But the lawyers told me I had no option.

At that age you figure nothing can go so wrong that hard work and the right attitude won't get you out from under it. I had Dad's and a lot of other blokes' examples to follow. They'd hung in there during the eradication years – so could I now. I didn't want to listen to lawyers' advice. I wanted to walk away clean with no debts behind me like a bad smell for the rest of my working life.

Then, to really rub my nose into it, a story came out in one of the local newspapers about the company and Troy Dann owing a supplier $15,000. Here I was with my name being splashed all over as a bad risk. I was humiliated, and the

word going round was that I'd gone under. I felt I had embar-
rassed my family.

Up until then, when things had gone wrong in my life,
there'd always been the sense that tomorrow was another day.
A brand new day, with yesterday's hard lesson learned that
would equip me better to deal with the next challenge. I'd
always felt that, however rough things got, there was a way
ahead. But bankruptcy, and the public exposure of failure,
when I wasn't even entirely responsible for the debacle, really
got to me. In the end, though, I had no one to blame but
myself!

It was the first time I realised that there are people who'll
actually take pleasure in watching someone else brought
down. I don't know whether it's envy or jealousy or just
plain stupidity that makes people find somebody else's setbacks a cause for celebration. But I do know that people
who live their lives to crow about others' problems and disappointments aren't living at all. Life is about getting out
there and doing, taking risks, looking after your family, your
mates, people who look to you and rely on you the way
you do to them as the wheel turns. Nothing in life is certain:
you can't take a thing for granted and, as a philosopher once
said, sitting in his bath or standing underneath a tree
somewhere – life's a bitch.

As if to grind that universal shard of philosophy in, I was
about to have another unfortunate encounter with reality, and
lose a great little mate along the way. But, in the end, even
coming on top of my humiliating bankruptcy as it did, it
actually better equipped me to deal with the whole disastrous
episode, and move on smarter, clearer eyed and more aware
of my place on this earth.

I was working at Mistake Creek, and there was a full day
of mustering ahead of us. Dad was in the bull catcher, most of
our stockmen were out on horseback, a couple were in trucks,
and I was in the fixed wing, M.L.P., with a chopper along for
the job, as well. I'd just taken the plane back from a 100-hourly
service. Any pilot will tell you that the most dangerous time
to fly a plane is straight after a service, because you never know
what the mechanic might have done to cut corners or over-
looked in a careless moment.

You don't really need to talk to a pilot about this. Most of
us reckon our car never comes back from routine logbook
services the way it went in. Well, imagine that the vehicle
concerned is 150 metres off the ground when some bolt falls
off somewhere. You're not on terra firma with a pull-over lane
alongside you.

I did all my checks of the plane with the chopper pilot,
Pete Mitchell, there with me. He was flying the helicopter that
day, a Robinson 22, and the machines were side by side as we
both went through the necessary pre-flight checks. I did all my
water drains, shaking my wings to help empty out any water
to the draining points that might have got into the fuel tanks.
Water can get through the top of the fuel cap if it's not sealing
well, but it's heavier than fuel so it will settle on the bottom
where the drains are. The tanks themselves are bladders, and
there are many sneaky ways that water gets itself into places
you don't want it. I put my full body weight on the tail of the
plane to lift the plane's nose and thus drain any water out of
the top wings.

It was lucky Pete was there because I used his sight glass to
check the fuel, and it came up 100 per cent after the water
drains, so I felt there were no problems lying in wait there. I

waved him away after that, because the plan was to join him out on the job. He'd have been gone five minutes by the time I taxied out and took off, the plane flying sweet as always.

I'd flown maybe a kilometre from the strip, where the terrain turns rough with lots of little creeks eroded into the ground by run-off from the nearby hills. There were trees scattered all over it, spear grass and rubber bush trees as well, so it wasn't flat and it wasn't clear, but I'd flown over the area enough not to be too worried by any of that.

I'd got up enough air speed to release the last 20 degrees of flaps, but the instant I did it, the engine cut out. Just stopped. Put these two things together and it's a simple sum with one result — I was falling out of the sky very quickly.

You only have seconds to decide what to do and no training can give you the experience. All the same, the training I'd had kicked in quick, and I started gliding the plane down for the clearest patch of ground I could see. There wasn't a lot of choice, and I had nothing like fingertip control here. Talk about wings and a prayer! I had maybe 100 metres of altitude to go with, so it definitely wasn't play time. The slope of a hill ahead of me was pretty clear of scrub, mainly grass, but it was a slope, which meant I was about to stop hard and fast.

There was no time to think about that. All I could do was try and get as much control over a bad situation as I could. I tilted the nose back up after reaching my best glide speed to give me as much time as possible before hitting. Moving forward, I kept the plane at some degree of straight and level, booting in the right rudder at the last minute to avoid three big trees and dropping like a stone!

Ten metres or so off the ground, I tried to get some flare

going to pull back on the plummeting speed I was making. I had the control column pulled hard back into my stomach – 9, 8, 7, 6, 5 metres – then she finally responded. The little beauty, she gave me some back, and even though my eyes and brain were telling me that the ground was coming up at me faster than I ever wanted to see it, M.L.P. was just that little bit lighter in my hands, giving me enough control to put her down not exactly where I wanted but where I had no choice.

No more time to think. We hit the ground, teeth rattling, knees slammed forward into the dash. But the belt held. As we bounced and slid forward across the ground, small rocks and dirt hit the windscreen. I was expecting the worst, that what was to follow would be the earth coming straight through my body and taking me to a place only the dead know. I was counting the seconds down, then the terrain changed from grassed soil to a patch of rocks in a small gully.

The front wheel collected the first of the rocks. The plane bent forward then flipped over. I watching those rocks coming closer, like the earth was falling out of the sky on to me because I was slowly turning upside down.

Cccrruuunnch. The plane landed on its roof, me head over heels in it, still in my seat with the harness holding tight. But all I could think of was those full fuel tanks blowing up. I'd seen enough movies and knew how, if they'd ruptured and caught a spark with the power still on, I was done for. I hadn't had enough time to shut the power off on impact, so all I was thinking was, 'Turn them off! Turn them off!' I reached below for the dash but couldn't reach it. I was sure I was history. I pulled the harness catch loose, dropped to the roof and shut off the power. Kicking the door open, I scrambled out and ran

along the wing and kept going a good 50 metres or so off the
end of it before I stopped and turned around.

I couldn't control myself. I started laughing. There was
M.L.P., upside down on the slope side. But I wasn't laughing
at the pathetic indignity of her last resting place. I was laughing
because I was alive. Against all the odds of what had really only
been the last two minutes of my life but had seemed to be
happening both in a few sped-up seconds and like a horrible
nightmare lasting hours, I was out. On my own feet, breathing
pure fresh air and not petrol-soaked flames, without too much
more to show for the danger I'd just passed through than two
cut up knees.

I was only about 7 kilometres from the station, so an hour's
walking brought me back, where I found Dad moving the bull
catcher out of the shed.

'What're you doing here, mate?' he asked. Obviously I
wasn't looking any worse for wear for the morning's disaster.

'I've crashed the plane,' I said. 'The motor stopped on me.'

Dad just grinned like I was taking the mickey out of him.
He wouldn't believe me, but in the end he came around, and
we drove out to the crash site.

When he saw M.L.P. the way she was, he looked at me
deadpan. 'Just what deal have you done with the devil to come
through the scrapes you do?'

'Reckon it's got more to do with the Good Bloke, Dad.
He must have plans for me.'

'Obviously,' he said.

Whatever plans the heavens might have had, the next stage
involved an investigation of the crash by the authorities and a
visit from the insurance company. It turned out that there was
a design fault in the double fuel-line system which had built

up enough deposits of rust and water in the little plane's carburettor that it was only a matter of time before the fuel jets clogged, the engine went dry, and the little plane couldn't fly. The insurance company paid out on the claim as the accident was put down to a plane fault rather than pilot error. You live and learn.

The whole story of my experience was written up in *Aviation Digest*, which concluded that the only thing that had saved me was my piloting, getting it right, and commending me for the cool-headedness I'd shown under duress. Nobody could turn down a rap like that. But I kept to myself that a whole lot of Lady Luck, some quickly remembered prayers and maybe, just maybe, whoever it is that watches over us, had as much to do with it as my piloting skills.

So, in a short space of time I was made to look like a dunce and even a rogue in one paper and held up as a positive example of skill and cool-headedness in another. It was a lesson, something I remembered a few years down the track when I was working in television and had suddenly become 'public property': never believe your own notices. Instead, focus on what you've actually done, recognise what you know you wish you could do again and do better and keep moving.

Just the same, keep your good clippings: your grandkids might want to see them one day. The other ones the cat can read this afternoon.

CHAPTER 20

....

SHANNON

I might have survived a plane crash, but I was still hurting from the article about my financial problems. Life's hard enough as it is without spite helping things along.

But while I no longer had the plane, M.L.P., I still had Shannon, my beautiful quarter horse. If there's any bond I rank up there with family and loved ones, it's the bond between a person and the animals they work with. I've had great companionship and terrific working support from both dogs and horses in my years working the Outback, but there was never a horse quite like Shannon. Those first years getting to know each other, working like we were one brain, one set of muscles, one pair of alert eyes, I wouldn't swap for however much tea there might be in China, or gold in the hills.

Much as I loved Shannon, I still had that love for speed and hard riding that only a motor bike could give me on the ground. So Shannon got some spell time, which meant she'd be out in the horse paddock without seeing me for a month, maybe two. But when I came out to get her, anyone anywhere, whether they'd seen a horse in their lives before or not, could see that we loved each other. Shannon would come straight up to me, looking at the bike I'd ridden out on like it was some poor smelly little racket maker and that was the end of its abilities. Then she'd look at me like my mother, as if I must be mad getting on the thing. If I really wanted to cross some country, really get the job done right, then she forgave me for being away so long and turning up with my rowdy, stink-making bike, because she was ready to work.

One morning, I was out on my motor bike checking the bores while I tried to figure out how to solve my financial problems so I wouldn't have to declare bankrupt. I found some tracks from a four-wheel drive vehicle on a road. They went right through one of our fences. It happens a bit in the bush right around the country: people trespassing, driving vehicles with off-road capability, being stupid and totally careless about other peoples' property and sometimes harming the natural environment.

If rangers catch people who do this they can slap a fine on them, but there's always another idiot who doesn't think things through before they plough across someone's livelihood. It's plain stupidity, the kind that most of us have done on occasions, and which still make us blush and wonder what we were thinking and if our brains were in idle at the time.

But what I was to find as I followed these tracks were not examples of stupidity or plain dumb carelessness. It was mindless cruelty, undertaken coldly and with such vicious lack of concern for living things that it still makes my blood boil.

About 5 kilometres in from the busted fence I found the first victim. One of our top stud bulls, dead from wounds to the stomach and legs. He'd been shot by a high-powered rifle, but shot where there'd have been no quick death for the poor beast. He'd have died slowly, suffering through it. I'm not a crying man: my tears come when they do because there's no other reaction possible in anyone with human feelings, but they don't turn on like tap water. I know what pain is, I recognise pointless suffering, but I live in a world where Nature's red tooth is just a beat away, whether it be a lunging snake, a fall from a horse, a vehicle rolling over on its driver or a gun accidentally firing. Believe me, on the land you exist with danger at your side, and it's every individual's responsibility to know that, and behave to keep every-day accidents to the minimum.

But looking down at that bull, I could feel my tears pricking, for the waste, the anguish, for the pain of that beast. I was also building up a rage, because those tracks led on deeper into the paddock following many dead kangaroos. There was every chance with the eagles circling ahead that those tracks would lead to more victims, that I'd find other dead animals with vehicle tracks circling them over and over again as shots had been fired. Adding insult to injury, and perhaps explaining but never excusing the mindlessness, there were empty beer cans scattered there, too.

Then it hit me hard where those tracks might lead, because this paddock was currently holding a plant of station horses, among them my own little quarter horse mare, Shannon.

I sped the bike after those tracks, the smaller gauge of my bike's tyres square down the middle of the four-wheel drive's larger wheels. But there was nothing I could do to erase the path these people had made, nor where it led to and what I found.

They'd pulled up just short of a water trough, where the amount of hoof marks showed some ten or twelve horses must have been minding their own business, drinking. As station horses, they'd have been used to vehicles nearby, and might have looked towards the latest arrivals but, after a moment or two of curiosity, they'd have returned to drinking.

They'd have been sitting ducks, trusting, quiet and ignorant of the threat. They wouldn't have had a chance. But some guardian spirit of horses must've given that small mob just the hint of a chance, because spooked they'd obviously been, spooked into running clear of the vicious men with their cowardly gun. They'd made it, they'd escaped, terrified and running but free, far from the reach of cruel stupidity.

All but one.

Shannon lay stone still beside the trough, a bullet hole clean into her skull.

I'd grown up on PowderPuff, but he'd come to me a fully grown horse with a mind of his own and ways that had been set by many riders before me. But Shannon was all mine. I'd broken her in myself and we shared a partnership working out in the paddocks, camp drafting, cutting in the yards. She was a good polo horse, too. There weren't many things a rider could do with a horse anywhere that Shannon and I couldn't do together. She was so smart and responsive, as if she knew, without being asked, exactly what needed doing, even if she'd never done it before.

If you could say a horse took conscious joy in life, sharing with me the same sense of exhilarating fun in getting things done well and to the best of our abilities, then Shannon was that horse. She knew what she was doing. She didn't just do it at the tug of a rein or the touch of a boot, she was thinking it through, working on what she'd done before, and finding new ways to get it done better and as quickly as, if not quicker than, I sometimes thought, the bloke in her saddle. A partnership: that's what it was, years in the making. And now that had been ripped away from both of us.

I told a little lie back there – I am a crying man when it comes to family, and that includes those animals that become as close to me as human flesh and blood. In many ways a true animal can be closer to you than other people, as we humans tend to have different things on our minds to constant loyalty and support.

All I know is that looking down at Shannon I felt such hurt, pity, anger, blood-boiling rage, disbelief, shock – so many emotions were racing through my body – I don't know if I screamed out loud or not, because everything merged into the same frustrating cocktail of feelings I feel right now as I recall that day.

What I can tell you is what I did next. I sat there, patting her wither, which still had the faintest hint of warmth. As I looked at the churned mud of the four-wheel drive's tracks, and more beer cans littered there, with my hand on her side I calculated that they'd been there maybe seven hours before. They'd gone on their murderous spree under cover of darkness, like cowards everywhere. But no matter how I tried to think it through and work it out, I couldn't understand any of it. I was confronting sheer callous viciousness, and with tears on my cheeks I was too stunned to move.

If that vehicle had been there, if I'd caught the people who'd done this, I'm quite sure I'd have done something that

I might not have come to regret, but which would certainly have put me behind bars. I never had the chance to find out. It was their good luck – or mine, the jury can stay out on that one – because I never did find out who did it.

What I did discover in me was a potential for bloody violence I reckon is dormant in every one of us. I'm just grateful that I've never found out what would happen if that potential was unleashed. I hope it never is. I wish it never was in any human being. Unfortunately, we all know how often it is, and the horror that follows.

I cremated Shannon later, and spread her ashes around the paddock. So somewhere – you might say everywhere – she rides the Outback wind, free forever. In my heart, sometimes, I still ride with her.

It had been a bad time: the bankruptcy, almost meeting my maker in M.L.P., and then the best little horse I've ever had senselessly slaughtered. If ever I've had a testing time in my life, this was it. There was nothing for it, however, because the sun was still coming up, I still had breath in my lungs, blood in my heart and a whole lot else I wanted to do with my life. Obstacles are things you see when you take your eyes off your goals!

The family came through, as I know they always will, just as often loud in their support as they were quiet in it, seeming to know when best to leave me to myself and when I needed some close company. My closest friends were the same, seeing me through the bad patches that popped up, making sure I didn't have too bad a time when those chances came around, as they always do, because if life does anything, it goes on.

···

CHAPTER 21

THE OUTBACK LEGENDS

Working on the station, I could throw myself into what I knew needed doing, but I was never going to earn enough money to service my debts that way. Thoughts kept jumping up and tapping me on the back of the head, but most of them were just a little too far-fetched. Then suddenly I realised I'd already done the groundwork for something that just might work out: music.

My dad's brother, Uncle Scottie, had been voted South Australian Entertainer of the Year in the eighties, singing and slinging guitar all around Australia and afield. He was teaching his daughter Samantha to sing, and their talent was strong enough to have a very popular act doing the rounds. I reckoned that talent might just stretch across to my side of the family, too, so I formed a band with Brett, my old partner in showbiz crime, who could sling a fair guitar himself.

You see, singing and playing instruments is pretty much

second nature to people working long periods out on the swag. You reach the end of the working day, the campfire's going, billy's on the boil, some good big steaks are on the barbecue grill, potatoes are in the fire's edge ashes, and the next thing you know, guitar's in hand, harmonica's on your lips and voices are raised in song. These sessions might last long into the night, and who knows if the cattle stay in close to listen or just can't work out how far they'd have to go to get some peace.

Whatever the cattle might be thinking, we'd all be telling bush poetry or singing, kids and grown-ups, with the glow of the campfire on our faces and a song book that reached out to all the great songs, old and new, that tell of the working life, Outback style.

But not everyone can get out to that famous middle of nowhere (which is always somewhere, because that's where you are), so I reckoned we could bring the campfire to town, in a way: sing those songs and create that warm atmosphere closer to the audience's homes and well-sprung beds.

We called the band the Outback Legends. With a rhythm section, lead guitar and steel guitar – five musos in all – we went on tour to places very few people had ever visited. We went to thirty-plus Aboriginal communities and homelands, some of them places where not many white people would have been before. We travelled throughout the Northern Territory, across to the West Australian border, down to the South Australian border, meeting people who still don't even speak English, people with roots in this country tens of thousands of years standing.

Do you want to know something? Every place we went we were welcomed, and once we started playing, no common language, strangers to each other's eyes, well, all of that disappeared and the music did the talking. It was a magic time in my life, and after all the troubles I'd been through, it was healing as well.

We were driving two four-wheel drives, each with a caravan on the back, and it still amazes me some of the places we got to with those caravans. Even becoming bogged on 20-metre sand dunes couldn't stop the Outback Legends moving on to the next community 300 kilometres along the track, to the next gig, to the next bogging sand dune. But we never stopped moving, seeing parts of the country I haven't seen since. I sincerely hope that in some of those place we are actually remembered fondly as friends.

The tour lasted six weeks, and I'd figured I could clear maybe fifty or sixty thousand dollars by charging five dollars a head entry on top of the T-shirts and hot dogs we were selling. It was a travelling music and entertainment show.

Most of the communities we visited received their royalty cheques every fortnight, so very few of them happened to be cashed up when we'd hit, and entry fees were on the spot. At most places we'd arrive as cash had dried up, so we'd do IOU deals where they'd send the entrance fees back to Amburla's post office box. Nothing too unusual in any of that – a trust system – and I was happy to work the shows and the books that way. We just got by on fuel, and lived pretty rough.

The trip was wild and a real eye-opener to most of the crew along for the ride, especially the two girls, Samantha and Angela. They couldn't believe how the bulldust out there gets into everything. You can't brush it out or shake it out – it's always there, in your clothes, in your equipment, in your hair, everywhere.

It was a large group of us on that first Outback Legends

tour, and while I had little reason to doubt the money could be made, it wasn't how things turned out. I never actually received any of the IOUs for the shows we'd played, so by the time I'd met all the costs and wages for the trip, I was worse off than when we went out. A lot worse off financially, but somehow I was strangely re-energised so that I felt I could take on the world again. There's a spiritual energy out here that is unbelievable. Trust me!

Plan B was suggested by the band's bass player, Lee. He was as good as his word and came up with $10,000 to form a partnership to take the Outback Legends to Tamworth, the capital of Australian country music. We arrived as unknowns, played some gigs and by the last of our six shows, at the Service Club, word had got around that what we did was entertaining and featured good dancing and high-energy fun all built around an Outback theme, so we packed out the venue.

We were back in the hotel, after Tamworth '93, when I took a call from Lee Kernaghan, who's since become Australia's leading country music star, but at the time was just stepping up to that status with the word around he was due to win a Golden Guitar, the Academy Award of Aussie country music.

Lee was about to make a video for a song of his called 'Boys from the Bush', and was having a bit of trouble finding boys who looked like they'd been anywhere near the bush. He asked me whether the crew and I could join him for the filming or, at the very least, lend them our hats, which he reckoned were authentic enough to make anyone wearing them look like the real thing right down to their boot tips.

'Well, mate,' I said, 'it's a cowboy's rule, you can't take a bloke's hat. You can take his tucker box and his swag, maybe his woman, but you can't touch a bloke's hat. That's a rule of the bush.' There was a pause on the end of the line.

Then Lee said, 'That blonde I saw you with, mate . . .'

He'd taken me up on the joke, and both of us were laughing out loud. It was the start of a friendship, both professional and social, that's lasted through to this day, and has plans for both of us well into the next century.

Scottie, my uncle, Brett and I ended up doing the clip with Lee and his band, and it included a couple of ideas of my own that ended up on a television set near you. But the whole Tamworth adventure had totally cleaned me out – I had barely two dollars to rub together. It had been fun and it had given me an idea that music might be another element in the voice of the Outback that I was putting together, but it hadn't solved my financial problems.

So when Lee invited me to join him on the car trip down to Sydney, I reckoned it was the best idea I'd heard for a while. Sydney was the place I needed to be to start moving some of the script ideas that Brett and I had put together and to make the contacts I was going to need in the film and television industry. But I kept coming up against the same reaction, along the lines of, 'Yeah, good script, mate. Leave it with us. You're just a cowboy, stick to your horse, we'll take it from here.'

Yeah, well, boy from the bush with the authentic hat or not, I knew that was no way to do what I wanted to, just giving away the result of years of dreaming and work to so-called experts. I've got nothing against people with more experience than me in any field pointing out pitfalls or making suggestions, but when it comes to 'driving' a project, if I'm not the bloke behind the steering wheel, then why bother in the first place. You hire experts for advice, not to elbow you sideways.

The main idea I'd always had, whether it was through the feature film script, *Outback Legend*, or another idea that was creeping up on me – a television adventure documentary series – was to showcase Australia in all its diversity and beauty: its flora and fauna and its people as individual, interesting characters.

I knew that the people in the cities only had very sketchy ideas, beliefs and prejudices, even, about life in the Outback. I also knew most Australians in some strange way considered the country outside of the cities to be the 'real' Australia. But that 'real' Australia was a hodge-podge of those sketchy ideas, beliefs and prejudices. It wasn't real at all. I knew – I'd lived it for real.

I reckoned that if I could bring some of that knowledge to the city audience, I'd be doing them a good turn educationally and in pure entertainment value. I also figured that the whole package could become part of their own lives, in the sense that Australians do see themselves as still connected to the bush. Through a television show or film, a link could be made that the audience could decide to follow out into the real Australia, or not. But after they'd seen what I could show them and the rest of the world – the truth about the bush – there wouldn't be any of those bad joke ideas and country-hick stereotypes left standing.

That was the game plan but, for the moment, after I'd met Lee's whole family and had a great weekend with those really fine people, reality meant wiring home to a friend for just enough fuel money to get myself home.

I made it on the legendary last drop, after a trip that started out all those weeks before, first to places no one had ever been before, then on to the country's number-one country music fair, when Tamworth's population trebles, then down to Sydney, the gateway to Australia and, with my feet barely touching the ground throughout, back to Amburla.

I was still chock-full fired up to get *Outback Legend* moving, so I made some calls to neighbours on adjoining properties, pitching them the idea and asking them to invest. That brought in $35,000, enough seed money I'd been assured by some blokes on the far end of some other phone calls – film producers based in Queensland who I'd met on my travels – to get the famous ball rolling and the cameras soon after.

The next phone call was from those blokes, telling me they'd exhausted the 30,000 I'd sent them but still couldn't get any interest in the film, so they were bailing out. I realised, if the message hadn't already sunk in, that there was only one person I could turn to, to get these dreams of mine moving and stick with them all the way through. He may not have been such a pretty picture in the mirror first thing in the morning, but at least I could look him in the eye.

It was down to me. I had to be the film's producer if I ever wanted to see it made, and see it the way I saw it, and finally see it in cinemas all around the world. Of course, nobody makes a film or enters any large-scale enterprise all on their own, so I got together with Brett again to nut out our next move. We decided we'd use that final $5000 to finance a trip east, where we'd knock on every door we could find with the word 'film' on it: Film Victoria in Melbourne, the New South Wales Film and Television Office in Sydney and then up to Film Queensland in Brisbane.

Time was tight because the local season was about to start, when we'd be flat out working on the properties, and on top of that my bank manager was on my back every day. But we'd have one last crack at it. This was it. We made the trip, and ended up back in Sydney, having heard pretty much the same 'Cowboys, stick to your horses', line up and down the east coast. Along the way, we'd been tracked down and my car was repossessed to pay some of those debts. Brett hocked his guitar but soon we were at our lowest ebb, in a budget hotel in Bondi with no money to pay the bill, not even enough for a feed and with nothing to show for ourselves except, in my case, an Akubra hat.

We went down to a couple of the beachfront takeaway cafes and I offered to swap my hat for a couple of meals. But we were knocked back; there was nobody interested in that deal. Then we came across a Greek bloke in a giros shop, who tried on the hat. It fitted him perfectly, and he figured he was John Wayne himself. He looked the part, too, so he gave us a couple of giros and a can of coke each. Not a shred of lettuce was wasted, I can tell you, which was just as well because we didn't eat again for the next two days.

This still left a hotel room and the trip home to finance. Unfortunately, it also left my pride and joy motor bike, a Honda XR250, at home. I rang up the bloke who owned the motor bike dealership in Alice and told him he could have the bike for $3000, a thousand shy of its true value, if he'd transfer the first thousand dollars through to me in Sydney. He went for the deal, Brett and I went home, and the XR250 went into his front window.

I was home, sweet home.

CHAPTER 22

HARD YAKKA AT FREGON

There was a bitter letter or ten from the bank and other debtors informing me that my accumulated debt was hovering around 200,000 dollars. It was a nice round figure, like a millstone that can be admired for its curves anywhere except around your neck!

Well, I was too proud to ask anyone, especially my family, to sort out my problems.

What we'd set out to do with the company was so sensible that I couldn't see how anyone else would want to put up barriers to the plans we had for the harbour, for Darwin, flowing on from that, and for the Territory in the long run. Speak to any inventor, anyone with a big idea, and you'll find variations on the same sad tale. It can take a long time for the penny to drop loud enough for the whole world to hear it, and by then the bloke with the original idea may well be dead or so far gone he never even finds out it's been put into operation.

Then there's the bloke who has a great idea, gets the go ahead, even has most of the thing up and a long road towards running, and the carpet's pulled out from under him. There's an Opera House in Sydney I've heard about ...

Now, maybe it's something about Australian harbours that brings big ideas undone, I don't know, but the dredging company was definitely sunk, and even though many of the ideas and intentions I had way back then have since been moved on by others – and I reckon good on them, too – right then, having returned from the long trip to Sydney, I had to come up with something to get myself back in the black.

Some wise people say everything happens for a reason, and that every step we take, however way back down the track it might be, however unnoticed it might have been at the time, can change your life later. I've had enough evidence of that sort of turnaround in my own short years to know that it's true what they say.

I was talking through with Dad just what options I had to climb that mountain of 200,000 slippery dollars, when a phone call came through from Fregon. Fregon is an Aboriginal community just over the border in South Australia, south of the Musgrave Ranges.

While travelling through there with the Outback Legends, I'd had a chance to talk to some of the local elders, who were the owners of the station the homeland was on. These blokes were so happy to have the show in town, because lack of employment opportunity and a daily grind of heat and separation from the rest of the country had almost torn apart the local people. It was one of the saddest human tragedies I'd ever seen while I was there: thirteen- and fourteen-year-old kids staggering around with pannikins or cut off milk tins or whatever would hold the stuff – petrol – strung under their noses for easy sniffing.

Petrol sniffing was widespread among the young people of Aboriginal communities right across the country because the kids found out that by sniffing the stuff they could get so far away from their problems it felt like they'd never have to come back to them. For so many of these kids, that's exactly what happened, their minds ruined.

Since those dark days, many Aboriginal communities have worked to eradicate the problem, and have helped to save a whole new generation of kids from that plague. But the practice is still out there, just like city kids sniff glue or their parents drink, snort coke or smoke legally available tobacco products, for that matter. I wish I could say the latter insidious weed had never got its hooks into me, but as someone who's been battling cigarette smoking for some time, with success in sight, I could understand the frustration of the elders in the Fregon community as they watched their kids just die right there in front of them.

They had the same good idea a lot of people had before them. Give people work, work they could see the results of, have pride in, earn a living from and build up to pass on to their kids, then nine times out of ten people will stick at it and put dangerous distractions behind them. The work they had in mind was to get their station up and running with cattle and the large numbers of wild camels living there, which they were planning to develop for the tourist trade.

But the place had fallen into disrepair. A lot of land has gone back into Aboriginal hands over the past thirty years, but not a lot of management experience stayed on it or with it. That's a problem confronting everyone out here, because many people feel the lure of the city, or can't ever see themselves having a place of their own, or simply aren't interested in carrying on a family tradition that was never meant to be a prison sentence anyway. So there's a fairly constant drift of people from the land, and that's the way it's been for a long time. Technology has picked up some of the slack, with planes and helicopters, roadtrains and rail improvements and stud practices that have moved into in-vitro fertilisation, all of which have allowed less people on the ground to do the same job that many more hands did a generation ago.

The trouble is, a good management structure needs to be implemented and, as much as an Aboriginal stockman can ride and work stock with the best of them, running a successful property is another ball game with the pace of today's business world. You need business experience on your side to survive. All of the advantages of world practices are of no use if you don't know how to apply them or where to use them. That knowledge comes from experience and a never-say-die spirit. That's what we all look for, black and white, when we look out over a broad swathe of land and ask ourselves, what can this land give us in return for what we give it?

At Fregon they needed someone who knew what he was doing to get the infrastructure of the station to a starting point where the bigger plans could be put into operation. They needed fences repaired, yards built, water connected – the whole box and dice of a working station. And those elders had decided the bloke with the guitar and the big grin from the Outback Legends, who'd sat down with them the day after the show and made a lot of sense in what he was saying, he was the bloke they needed to get their station back on its feet.

Well, Brett wasn't available, so they settled for me. Gotcha!

As it happened, I did talk to Brett after the elders and I had worked out what they needed, and how much it was all going to cost and what equipment and supplies we'd need to get it done. But he was flat out with plans for his own place, so I called up a childhood mate of mine, Rex Allen, and proposed a fifty–fifty deal. Now I had a workmate for what was to prove some of the toughest work days of my life.

We packed up Rex's four-wheel-drive, throwing in the welder and all the fence-building equipment we'd need to build yards, and set out for what was to keep us hard at it for the next two months. Thankfully, there was no straying cattle on the roads running across under my wheels this time.

The station had really fallen into disrepair. The fences were down, the water supply systems damaged and the whole place needed picking up and dusting down. When we arrived, we got straight on to the jobs at hand. The first task was to build some camel yards for the beasts the community planned to bring in, break, and then sell on to tourist companies offering camel rides. There were companies running camel rides as far away as the beautiful beaches of Broome on the coast of north Western Australia as well as in Alice Springs and dotted right around the Territory, and they were all looking for good, clean animals they could take people out on for those swooshingly dusty rides that visitors can't seem to get enough of.

So the elders had done their homework. They knew the market they could service, and they were up and ready to do it. All they needed was the station infrastructure that would house, train and send on the camels already roaming all over it.

Rex and I were working in 50 degrees Celsius heat, with barely time to take in the fact that the country around us was starkly stunning, with its 15-metre sand dunes, amazing desert oak trees, hills on every horizon you looked to and the many small creatures skittering around under our feet. But, pretty as it was, both of us were due back in the Centre for the start of our own season up there, so the two months were tight and unrelenting.

I'd worked in hot conditions before, but this was punishing. In many ways I felt I was somehow due for it after all the mistakes I'd made in my life so far. Maybe, in the back of my mind I was thinking I could sweat out all my bad luck, and that persevering here would somehow prove I was up to any challenge a man could face. Leave out business partners, unpaid debts, patronising attitudes and I could do anything, I knew it.

So I worked hard, with Rex being a great mate who was there all the way beside me. We looked like wild dust devil men because we only got to wash our faces every couple of days and we were having to cart precious water in by hand. Showers or full body washes were out of the question, so I noticed we started working a little further away from each other every day. But the jobs got done all the same.

We lived in our swags and off canned food, the odd kangaroo or goanna adding some protein to the meals every now and then. There must have been plenty in the diet, because we put up two camel yards in pretty quick order.

Then we set up the station's bores, putting in troughs and tanks where they were best placed to service the movement of their animals, which, along with the camels, included both cattle and horses for more traditional mustering and sale to the market place.

By the end of the job, the place was set to go, and Rex and I had both made some good money. I had enough to service my debts, but that was all for the moment. The principal amount still loomed above me, six crushing figures that I hadn't quite figured out how to wipe clean.

I would wake up every morning determined to keep the long-term plans alive that sustained me: making the movie and having it go on to become a hit, write number-one songs with the band. And all the time aware that it was about keeping a shared dream alive, following in the footsteps of the likes of Banjo Paterson and Henry Lawson, to tell Australians stories about Australians then take them out to the wider world. But my first priority was to contribute to sustaining and enriching Australian culture as those blokes and many others had done before me.

People often say there isn't a real Australian culture, but I reckon in the 200 years that white people have been here, let alone the tens of thousands of years of Aboriginal occupation, this country's pioneers and ancestors of every origin laid the groundwork for the way we all see ourselves. Right now, Australians born and bred here as well as those more recent arrivals already so Australian you can't pick 'em from First World War diggers' great grandsons know what being Australian is. If there aren't quite so many people putting it into words these days, you can be sure there's a whole country living as Australians, being Australians and just getting on with the job.

That's how a culture is formed, by the way people live and work side by side, by the enthusiasms they share, the places they choose to live, the partners they make a life with and the children they raise and teach to value what's all around them. The job of artists, poets and film makers is to reflect all that back to us, until it becomes part of the whole picture and the

culture has one more facet, another tiny part of being Australian. That never stops – every minute of the day we're all
making our culture.

But it is the artists, especially people reaching out to a large
audience, these days via electronic media or moving pictures,
who can lead the way and shape the best of what's in us, and
warn us about what's worst as well as frame ways for going
forward. That's what I wanted to do, with every star picket
I drove into the ground, every wire I strained, every bore I
pulled to life-giving water below, every improvement that Rex
and I made to the station at Fregon.

And that was just one job. The same desire, the same
dream, was worked into everything I lifted my hand to, wherever I was, whoever I was working with or alongside. All the
debts, all the behind-my-back sniping, all the stupid cruelty
people could come up with, I was setting out to beat it, and
getting there every breath I took.

But the books I turned to next were the more prosaic
accounts that showed me, the Fregon job done, that I had
enough to get through the next three months. Five hundred
dollars here, 1000 there, another 500 to somebody else, all the
arrangements I'd made to pay off my debts, and slowly, slowly,
work my way back to the black. I didn't have a clue how I
was going to keep the payments up after those three months.
But not long after I returned home it was mustering season.
And that would take all my energies.

CHAPTER 23

THE FUTURE'S IN MY HANDS

Dad was running the season up at Mistake Creek, while I handled things at Amburla. I had good staff around me, not least Steve Anderson and Gail, a girl who'd come over from Queensland, so I was among friends. The jobs that needed doing I'd done before so I was also on familiar ground. I think that's one of the most important things you can have going for you when everything else seems to be against you – something familiar you can anchor yourself to so you can weather the storm. It might be a job, your family, a place or even an idea that you won't let go, so long as you have something you can call on that doesn't let you down. Even though I've had more lonely nights than most, I'm grateful for the support I got from my family and my mates during those tough times, and it's a real pleasure to be able to say that the few people who stuck with me then are still around now.

Out of the blue, I received a letter from the Northern Territory Department of Industries and Development. It came from a friend, Sue Shearer, who was head of the department in Alice Springs. She recommended that I write a submission for an award in the 1994 Young Achiever of the Year, which was a government scheme set up to recognise and draw attention to the work and community contributions of younger Territorians. The scheme had actually been advertised on television just a few nights earlier, and it caught my eye then as an idea. But I didn't think there was much in it for me, with the way the last year had gone until Mum rang and suggested I should put in the application to get exposure and for the chance to meet the right people with connections in the business world.

Steve and Gail also reckoned whatever else had happened on the down side of my ledger, I'd been in there having a go. And besides, when they started pointing out the things that hadn't gone belly up, I realised that there had been a lot of good in the last period, even if it was the disasters that had been weighing heaviest on my mind. So I did a submission, putting down what I'd achieved, all the work I'd put in to the properties, including the championship winning animals we'd had from the stud and the tourism activity that I'd begun which featured Amburla. As I was writing it, and going back over the years, at twenty-seven I realised that I'd packed a fair amount into a short time.

The department had been behind me on a couple of trips to Asia that I'd self-financed to promote the live-beef trade of our animals to that part of the world. This was in the very early days of what has since become a large part of the cattle industry in the Territory, and even though all of today's success didn't flow from my trips alone, every shoulder to that wheel had moved it along a bit.

These trips must have impressed the department as I was chosen, along with a handful of other Territorians, to represent our state as part of a special envoy to Asia. The seminars we attended there were to better understand their cultures and to work towards the future development of our foreign trade.

On a lighter side, I was developing a song-writing partnership with Lee 'Legend' Kernaghan, following on from our first meeting in Tamworth. Apart from the amount of money a successful entertainment enterprise can generate, it was also part of my wish to have some home-grown songs and stories about living on the land. One of those songs went to the top of the country charts, so anyone could see that something of Territory life and spirit was reaching a wide audience through that connection.

I also put in that I was developing a feature film to promote tourism and industry with the long-term aim of establishing a film-making infrastructure and policy in the Territory that would be competitive with any of the services offered elsewhere in Australia. And what a back lot!

My dream then – and it still is today – was to help the Aboriginal people work the land as successfully and economically as days gone by, for their independence, their future and their children.

All of it went in, including being nominated a year earlier for the Queen's Trust, a forum held in Western Australia involving young Australians deemed to be potential future leaders. I suppose if you were to read that submission now it would be pretty much a blueprint for many of the plans and activities that I've since begun. The exercise was also valuable because in writing about what I'd done and how I saw all of it moving forward, I got everything straight in my own head.

And you know something? Everything there I knew could be done. Putting it all down in black and white, even the dreams and tinsel of film making, made this cowboy who should stick to his horses realise that everything I wanted to do wasn't just wishful thinking, it could all be achieved in the real world, with all that anyone or anything could throw at me.

Still, sending off the submission, I wasn't too confident I'd done much more than write myself a letter spelling out the ten-year plan. I always think that an award should go to some other person who really deserves it. I'm not being falsely modest, but when you do what you do the way you always have, it's done, that's all. It's the other person beating the odds that always impressed me more and left me in awe. They deserved an award. Me, I was just plugging along trying to get as much out of life as I could. Getting passionate about it, treasuring the journey and growing stronger with the darkest hours, knowing there was always someone out there worse off than me. Because that's the only life I know.

The submission was long sent off in the post. I was days away from the end of that third month that my account books had told me I would come up against empty handed. I'd actually made a little extra from the station to tide me over another couple of weeks, but the walls of that tunnel were closing in on me, and the light at the end of it? Way out of sight.

An invitation came through to attend the awards ceremony, so I went up to Darwin and Mum and Dad joined me from the property for the evening, along with my Nana, my Auntie Helen, my cousin David and a good friend, Adam with his partner, as well as family friends Maria and Ken Pervis. There, along with everyone who was anyone in the

Territory, was Marshal Perron, the Chief Minister of the
Territory and a good man. So I said g'day to him and then
we sat down for the evening. It was a formal affair, the way
these things go, with everyone looking their best, and a lot
of pride and excitement around because there were seven
separate awards: career achievement, sports, arts, industry and
development, and so on.

I won't keep you in suspense: I won the award from the
Department of Industries and Development, and I reckon you
could have knocked me down with a feather I was so surprised.
I was one of the seven winners, and then it came to the overall
Young Achiever of the Year. You know what's coming? Yeah,
I won that, too, which really brought the tears to my Mum's
and Nana's eyes. They were proud of me. Dad shook my hand,
squeezing harder than he had in a long time.

I felt on top of the world right then, but even in the middle
of it all I couldn't ignore the cold fact that I was still looking
down the same barrel the next morning. No money, no immediate way to make enough of it, and a lot of cap in hand
coming up to renegotiate my debt repayments. But before all
that the Chief Minister asked me what my next project was.

I told him that the film was the big one, but along the way
I had the idea for a television series that would really show off
the Northern Territory as it is, mainly through the flora and
fauna of the place, but getting around enough to meet people
from every corner of the region to show the rest of Australia
and the world just how people, animals and plants thrived in
a place that has so often been described as uninhabitable. And
to show the spiritual energy and majestic beauty of the
Outback.

I was told to bring something in on paper to the department

the following week, so I put together a prospectus for a program we called 'Outback Adventures' because, the way I saw it then, and still do, just living and working out here is an adventure. On top of that, visiting the place is as well. Nothing just happens in the Outback – it happens in a way that you can't help learning from, being educated by, or just feeling clean amazed by.

I reckoned we could show the world the place differently to the way it had been shown before. The prospectus clinched grants from the department as well as sponsorship from other sources, including the support of the Imparja television network, that totalled $35,000.

I pulled in a mate of mine who was already working on the station, Mark, and another mate who was a cameraman, Glenn Adumus (he calls himself 'Glenn of the Outback'). The three of us drove around the country filming sequences that would end up in a fifteen-minute trailer I named, 'Our Country'. I directed and produced, spent a whole lot of time in front of the camera and generally got down on videotape images of the land, flora and fauna and some of the daily activities involved in Territory life.

I was having a great time! Calling in mates so I could shoot from one helicopter to another for great aerial footage. Dropping in on family friends to film kids growing up, adults working and at play, animals moving through the scrub and across plains, fording creeks and filling yards and roadtrain trailers. Riding my horse, driving bull catchers, meeting great people and seeing beautiful sights.

We went to 'desert' country, through wetlands, along highways and down off-road tracks. We saw herds of cattle, mobs of wild horses, buffaloes, camels, feral pigs and donkeys.

We drove next to kangaroos hopping alongside us like escorts before all of a sudden bounding out of sight. We got bogged, a few flat tyres, got baked by midday heat and chilled by pre-dawn cold, met characters a scriptwriter couldn't get away with and watched tourists seeing things that made their jaws drop and me remembering how lucky I was to live where they were passing through. We kept moving, we kept filming, we kept to the schedule – a film maker's golden rule – we even kept to budget, a film producer's *iron rule*.

They were long days, but I felt that this was it, this was the start of what I wanted to do with my life. Everything I'd learnt, every skill and trick of my many trades, all the bits of Aboriginal survival techniques, locating bush tucker, turning up water from a dry creek bed, knowing what weather was coming in from the movement of animals and birds, the things my Dad and Mum and other people had shown me around a station and out on the swag, they were all coming together. I was in front of a camera, and sure enough about what I knew to turn to that camera and tell people who'd eventually be watching me that this was this and that was that. All the same, it wasn't easy being in front of camera – it's just that I couldn't find anyone else to show what I wanted.

What I didn't know I could ask a local wherever I went, and in the process I discovered how much natural talent there was out there. That first trip really brought home how big a canvas I was setting out to paint on, how many stories I could tell, pictures I could show, sounds I could bring into every Australian's living room. I'd spent much of the $35,000, and the footage would cut down to just a tight fifteen minutes. But what I really had was right there in my hands. It was my future.

CHAPTER 24

··

AN AKUBRA ON THE RIVIERA

That fifteen-minute pilot was edited, music put to it, titles and credits added till it was finally finished and ready to show. First up was a showing for family and friends, a 'world premiere' that went down as well as I could have hoped and then some. But 'Our Country' was never a home movie. It didn't look like one, it hadn't been made to be one, and it wasn't going to the bottom drawer of any cupboard of mine while I had breath to move it along.

I called Ross Dimsey, who was then head of Film Queensland, and who had given me support in the past.

'Mate, I'm not getting anywhere in Australia with this. Where can I show my production to the rest of the world?' I asked.

'M.I.P.C.O.M.,' he said, 'It's a film and television exhibition that's held annually in the south of France, at Cannes.'

It's not the famous film festival, which is about promoting finished feature films, but a showcase for upcoming television productions or shows that might be at the same stage as mine, with some demo or pilot material, and for which the producers are looking for backing to go to full production.

He told me M.I.P.C.O.M. was four weeks away, but I'd need to register and make arrangements to get myself there and get 'Our Country' into the program. I couldn't go on the Film Queensland slate because we'd never got far enough east to film anything in that state that might have helped the pilot qualify, but Ross offered to meet up with me there and show me the ropes.

I was paying my own way again, so I couldn't afford to stay on the Riviera at any of the $400-a-night hotels. I stayed at the Bronx, about 2 kilometres inland, which was worse than any backpacker place I'd ever stayed at, in a room not much bigger than a Territory pantry at $150 a night.

But I was there, with my videotapes and a flier to push the show. That wasn't going to be enough in a town flooded with tapes and posters, so I decided I'd present myself the way nobody would look twice at back home, but in the south of France just might draw some attention: Akubra hat, Driza-bone coat, R.M. Williams boots, looking about as Australian as I could and proud of it, without making a galah of myself. Sure enough, in rooms full of blokes in suits, I stood out from the crowd. And it was working!

I had a guidebook full of all the names of attending production companies. It was a sort of temporary bible for anyone wanting to do business there, and there was enough in it to keep you busy twenty-four hours of every day, so long as you read between the lines and remembered that the original Bible is full of parables and wisdom you have to think through and not always take at face value.

There were six other producers there from Queensland, and we'd get together for a coffee every now and then but, at base, it was everyone for themselves. M.I.P.C.O.M. attracts producers, broadcasters and network executives from all over the world. It's the international television production showcase of the year, so I wasn't just casually wandering from cafe to cafe, enjoying the Mediterranean air. I met with everyone that gut feeling told me might react positively to my ideas, my plan and the pilot tape. I was wearing through the soles of those R.M. Williams but getting some strong reactions as I went.

I can't say I was actually in my element – that's a place and a state of mind somewhere geographically central in the Great Southern Land – but I was having a good time and an energising time. It's a bit like working a mob of cattle – you have to develop a knack for sniffing out what's coming up next, getting yourself subtle to all the little signs so you can move ahead of the mob and push them where you want them to go. The problem was, there were a lot of other people with the same sort of skills and a bit more experience working the herd. But that didn't mean I couldn't have wins along the way, even if I was a jackaroo!

I'd had very solid interest from a New Zealand company, another based in Canada and an American company, so I was feeling pretty good about things. Good enough to sit down in a cafe and look out on the rest of the world with some certainty that at least one part of my dreams was shaping up. In case you didn't know, I'm a fairly positive person.

I was at my table when a bloke came up to me, like a lot of others had done before, reacting to the hat and boots.

'You from Texas?' It was the line I'd heard from most of them.

I was really proud to be an Australian in that part of the world, where huge companies like Disney and Warners were spending millions of marketing dollars to draw attention to themselves, while I was getting attention with a hat, a coat and some boots.

I'd tell the blokes who asked me if I was from Texas that Australia was the one of the last frontiers in the world and that was where I came from. If they hung around for a coffee, I'd tell them more. That was where the interest was coming from, people who responded to what they saw then got hooked on what I could tell them.

But this bloke, he should've known better, and I reckon he did as soon as I opened my mouth.

'No, mate, Australia,' I said.

'Ah, mate, so am I. But I've been over in America for a while.' His name was Fenton, and we sat and yarned for a while before he asked what I had with me. Believe me, you're not at M.I.P.C.O.M. without something to buy or sell on you, so anyone's safe getting straight to tin tacks.

I told him about the show idea, and he said he'd like to come on board, figuring he could help move the project. As in, ten minutes from then. Fenton had a meeting with the Becker Group, a company out of Australia best known in those days for their 'Man from Snowy River' TV series. But they were doing all sorts of other programs, too, and looking to expand their production slate.

'I've got them on my list,' I said, flicking open the M.I.P.C.O.M. bible I always had on me.

'Come down with me,' said Fenton. 'I'm meeting with a

bloke called Ian Hogg. I reckon he'd go for your ideas.'

It turned out to be a really good meeting. Ian Hogg, a smart, young bloke around my age who seemed really energetic, locked straight into my vision for the show. Here I was with an Australian, Sydney-based company and they were interested. In my heart, I'd always wanted to go with locals, as positive as those other three companies had been. It would have felt a little strange making a show about Australia with out-of-towners.

That was my second last day in Cannes, so the next day I caught a train out on the first leg of the long journey home, where I was back under my own roof, but flat broke again.

Three weeks later I still hadn't heard a word.

I'd had so many positive responses over the years about this and other ideas of mine and then have the whole thing come to nothing. I didn't want to even think it was going to be the same story all over again. But sitting out on my verandah alone, watching the sun set, with a dingo's howl or two out in the gathering darkness, there were occasions when I felt as low as a bloke can go without putting himself six feet under.

I was all churned up inside, feeling like the best thing I could do was have a good old bawl, cry my eyes out if that's what it would take to get all the tension lanced out of me. But, it's hard for a man to cry, or it was for me.

Everything people had said to me over the years about being pretty bloody good if I turned out half the man my old man was hung over me. I reckoned I wasn't turning out a tenth of what he was, a man who'd worked his way up from a blood-stained apprentice butcher's apron to owning and running properties all across the Outback. He'd got his family through droughts, a rural depression, the herd-gutting eradication program, enough setbacks and throw-downs to have broken six other men, but Garry Dann had pulled through a winner.

The last thing I saw was myself measuring up to him, sitting there, those dingo's howls sounding like mocking chiacking, telling me that all I was, was a dreamer, a cowboy who should stick to his horses, and I mightn't even be much chop at that!

....

CHAPTER 25

THE BIGGEST OUTBACK ADVENTURE YET

Down I was, but I wasn't about to spend too much time in those sorts of dumps. And proud as I was of my old man and the family name he'd given me, I had to make it myself, not just follow another bloke's lead.

It had been a tough year, though, and a lonely one. I'd been travelling around with a vision of myself as a director and a producer, knocking on doors in the film and television industry without too much idea of how to get everything up and moving. I knew that my eyes could see things in the Outback that most people wouldn't ever see – some of them couldn't see – until they were pointed out to them.

The certainty that I could deliver something pretty special for our country was still so strong that I never stopped writing the poems and the lyrics I'd been working on for years, getting down in words and music my special relationship with living and working where I did. I was still pushing *Outback Legend*, even though Brett had had to pull out, going back into the portable abattoirs on his family property.

It had been about a year on my own now, without too much contact with my friends because I was always travelling or working, but the wash-up was there hadn't been much time for socialising – or any money, for that matter. I really didn't know where I was going. The morning's were tough, knowing I had a job ahead of me, whether it was a muster or some fencing. I've always been an early riser, but on some mornings it was hard to jump out of bed.

All the time, though, I kept telling myself something had to happen. I couldn't put in all the effort and time and have the absolute conviction in my plans for nothing to come of it. There had to be a wheel somewhere, turning, slow as it was, around to me. Anyone who's ever had an idea, an invention, a belief, will know what I mean about the sense of complete loss that comes along and pulls the rug from under your enthusiasm and the belief and faith you have in yourself. Some people might think of it as a test to sort out the wannabes and the easy-way-outers from the people really sticking to their guns.

To keep me going I thought back over and over again to the pioneers of Outback history and settlement, reckoning that what those people had been through was a real test, often of life and death. I was lucky enough to be able to call on the strength of examples from my own family, even beyond the obvious examples of my own Mum and Dad to grandparents and great grandparents, great uncles who'd pioneered trails now laid out flat and hard for cross-country transportation, women who'd kept stations going while their men went out to meet head-on the challenges of a country tough and demanding as any on earth.

My family, my neighbours, there wasn't a mob in the Territory I could think of who hadn't had their backs up against the wall, and most of them had pushed off it to come back more determined than ever. These thoughts kept me going when the dreams and the ambitions weren't enough, because on their own they never are. Anyone can dream – it's making those dreams happen that sorts out the crowd in the yard, especially when 'dreams' are often fashioned from the same blood, sweat and tears as ordinary every-day work. The rewards, the prizes, the winner's ribbon, if they were given away, what use would they be?

But every tether has an end, and I was just about at the end of mine. The sparkling Mediterranean sun was a fading memory and the promises and hype of M.I.P.C.O.M. were turning into a bad episode of 'Dallas'. Then the phone rang.

Mum answered it. I was out pulling a bore that couldn't be put off.

I called Beckers back and they told me they liked my project, and wanted to talk deals as soon as I got myself down to Sydney. Yesterday, ideally. I was too broke to afford a plane ticket, so Mum and Dad picked that up, and I was on the plane and into their offices to cut a deal as soon as aeroplane schedules, my spinning head and the whole family's excitement had died down.

I was about to start out on the biggest adventure of my life up until then. I'd been exposed to more danger before. I'd had more demanding physical challenges confront me. Had to deal with as many complex demands on my time and skills. Been required in three places at once often enough.

Worked hard and seen long-developing plans slowly take shape.

But this was my dream turning into reality right here. The decade of writing, talking, sketching out ideas and stories, seeing pictures in my mind, sharing them and developing them with my closest friends – the opportunity had arrived to put it all into practice. To take what had been locked between my ears and place it before a vast audience, firstly in Australia and then right round the world.

Everything that I believed about the unique beauty of where I lived, the stunning geography, the fascinating flora and fauna, the character of the people resident here, the challenges, the rewards, the disappointments, the successes, the values, the stories of the Outback were all about to be told.

Through my eyes, with my voice, calling on friends, family and close and distant neighbours, to weave the tapestry of daily life, history and plans for the future in Outback Australia. To visit places that many would never be able to see anywhere but on their television screen and to inspire them to visit.

To record the struggles faced by people in one of the harshest, most cruelly beautiful environments on the planet, which, for all that, has sustained human beings for thousands of years and which is now productive both above and below the ground, offering fresh opportunity every day to its inhabitants, whatever their origin, to pursue their dreams and ambitions.

But also to show how other life continues to thrive here with remarkable diversity, life that manages to deal with drought, flood and extremes of climate that have wiped species out elsewhere. Plants with deep roots or bulbous trunks, both conserving access to water; fish that lay eggs in creek beds so that if drought should come and creeks dry, their eggs will eventually hatch, however long it takes for water to return; kangaroos that stagger the maturation of their offspring to ensure that there are always new young to carry on the species; frogs that hibernate through those long dry spells; birds that devise their own migratory tactics to avoid the worst excesses of an inhospitable climate.

There are so many small, life-threatening and life-preserving adventures going on in Outback Australia. With the television show I was about to make, the great adventure of the Outback and its spirit of survival, of adaptation to fresh challenges and the conviction out here that tomorrow will come and be met face on, was to be brought to an audience who, I hoped, would discover some of that Outback spirit in themselves. So people could see something uniquely Australian, and then understand that what they saw, Australian as it is, is really universal, the human spirit to go on, to not be beaten down, to survive, to thrive and to pass on the challenges to that next generation.

My dreams had come to something because I'd never let them go, and I'd never sold them short. I'd hung in there, I'd worked to make those dreams have a place in the real world, and I'd given them shape in words, on paper, in moving pictures. I had reached out to people with things they could listen to, look at, get a handle on. The lesson in this was that dreams have to be worked, made accessible and that, inspired as an idea might be, nothing gets conveyed by hot air alone.

To all my young friends out there, you can achieve anything you want in your life: it just takes hard work and a strong belief in yourself. It's up to you all to educate older Australians so we can bury the tall-poppy syndrome and get behind each other. Everyone has talents. We live in the greatest country in the world, so long as we remember that hand in hand with freedom goes responsibility.

You have a dream. We all do. I still have many ambitions, as yet unrealised, such as setting up a children's foundation in Outback Australia inspired by Jacob and my sister Tanya. I expect I'll still have ambitions on the day I take my last breath. I'd better have — it's certainly what I plan right now.

So, there are many more adventures to come. I plan to share some of mine with you. And I'd like to share in yours some day, somewhere.

EPILOGUE

Life *has* to be a test, and at your darkest hour, one big nightmare that never seems to end. But I'd have to be one of the luckiest blokes in the world. Because, in September 1997 my nightmare finally ended, and I signed a major deal in the television industry!

After three months of pre-production, we were set to go. I had asked my sister Simone to co-host the series with me, to which she readily agreed. I figured that to reach a large audience we needed to meet people from all walks of life. In addition, a lot of the unsung heroes in the Outback are women, so who better to do it than my wonderful sister Simone, a woman from the land herself! On top of that, we had to have *someone* on the show that was not only intelligent, but good looking as well!

To produce twenty-six one-hour programs of the magazine-style show I wanted, you need to deliver close to 200 separate stories. I didn't want the show to be classed as documentary, but more a lifestyle program with action, animals, and beautiful scenery to keep it all flowing. I knew that a few of the ideas I came up with were a bit over the top, but you make your own fun out here and we wanted prime time TV. It was a huge challenge we had set ourselves because, in my mind, I was never going to settle for a lesser time slot.

Everything we've done on 'Outback Adventures', I've experienced myself or with someone, somewhere, at some stage of my life!

I'm proud to say 'Outback Adventures' has gone on to be shown to millions of people in over 163 countries around the world, with over 250,000 hits on our web site per month, which promotes tourism and the characters in Outback Australia.

It's rewarding to learn via the many personal e-mails I get daily (mostly from Australia, America, and Europe) that people have been so inspired by the show or the web site that they're now saving up to come to Outback Australia.

The response I've received from young children, in particular, has blown me away. Never in my wildest dreams could I have expected this response from my own country, especially after everything I'd endured over the past ten years. If we've given some of our young Australians a window into Outback Australia, giving them pride in their forefathers and a strong belief in themselves and their heritage, then I've done the job I started out to do.

❖   ❖   ❖

In recent years, many classics have been made about the Wild West of America, which is claimed to be the world's last frontier. Outback Australia is four times as big as Texas and equally as beautiful. The Outback would now have to be one of the last frontiers.

The movie *Outback Legend* is now in production, and I'm hopeful it will be in cinemas by the end of 2000 to coincide with the Sydney Olympics.

Outback Legend is a feelgood movie with all the ingredients: action, adventure, love, heartache and drama. It's a strong family movie with the right morals and beliefs and without the bleakness of many movies today, which, to me, send the wrong messages to our youth. Teenagers will love the action, Australians the patriotism; Americans will love the landscape beauty and the sophistication of the story line; the Japanese will love the wildlife and animals; and Europe, all of the above!

Don't ever think that, once you've succeeded at what you wanted to do, it gets easy, because it doesn't. You'll meet many beautiful people in your travels, but there'll always be people who just want to use you or see you fail. Then they'll drop you like a hot cake before they keep their end of the bargain.

Don't ever let this put you off. Rise above them, because you're a better person than they are, and what goes around comes around, I believe.

You don't get anything out of life unless you put something back, either. That's why I'm proud to be launching soon a new Australian-owned dog food to help the 'Troy Dann Children Foundation' I've recently set up. Hopefully it will help lessen the suffering of many children and many parents, like my special sister, Tanya, and her husband, Steven.

We are now entering a new age, going into the new millennium, and although the simple things in life may have all but passed us, I feel we have many special dreams and journeys ahead. And you know what? I'm really excited about them!

GLOSSARY

bull catcher: a utility vehicle with roll bars used to muster wild cattle. Old tyres are strung across the front as padding for when some persuasion is needed!

chilpy: slang for elderly Aborigine

coach cattle: cattle that has been mustered previously and so more domesticated than wild cattle coming in to the herd

Codan radio: a two-way radio of the Codan brand name

Dreamtime: a spiritual belief concerning all living things on earth, usually handed down by Aboriginal elders

forcing pen: a small yard used to channel stock up the loading race

gidgee tree: a type of native tree

gilgai: a natural erosion formed by the contours of the land

jackaroo (or roo): an apprentice stockman

jillaroo (or roo): an apprentice stockwoman

knobby: a beast with no horns

mickey: a young weaner bull

mob: a group or herd

muster: gathering and putting together stock from a paddock into a stockyard, or moving stock from one paddock to another

Poeppel Corner: point at which the Northern Territory,

Queensland and South Australia meet

perenty: Australia's largest lizard, having many sharp teeth and being often well over a metre long

plant: mob of working horses

race: yard panels built parallel, approximately 1 metre apart, and used to guide stock single file onto a truck, draft or brand

to red-line: to travel at full acceleration

roadtrain: a truck (prime mover) carting stock and other produce, measuring up to 150 metres long with three trailers

station: a very large farm, or ranch.

wether: a male goat

windrow: V-type drains made off roads in usually a 45-degree angle allowing water to run off into the bush away from the road crown

witchetty bush: native bush

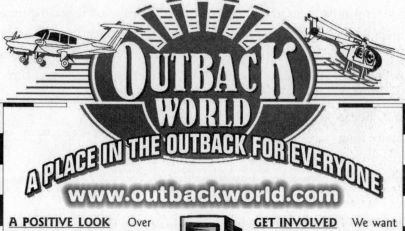